To Auntie
Much
Myr

Good-bye To My Favourite Aunt

Copyright © 2015 by Myrna Seagrave.

All rights reserved. No part of this publication may be reproduced, distributed, or transmitted in any form or by any means, including photocopying, recording, or other electronic or mechanical methods, without the prior written permission of the publisher, except in the case of brief quotations embodied in critical reviews and certain other noncommercial uses permitted by copyright law. For permission requests, write to the publisher, addressed "Attention: Permissions Coordinator," at the address below.

BookVenture Publishing LLC
1000 Country Lane Ste 300
Ishpeming MI 49849
www.bookventure.com
Hotline: 1(877) 276-9751
Fax: 1(877) 864-1686

Ordering Information:
Quantity sales. Special discounts are available on quantity purchases by corporations, associations, and others. For details, contact the publisher at the address above.

Printed in the United States of America

Library of Congress Control Number:		2015934622
ISBN-13:	Softcover	978-1-942703-57-0
	Pdf	978-1-942703-58-7
	ePub	978-1-942703-59-4
	Kindle	978-1-942703-60-0

Rev. date: 11/02/2015

Disclaimer

This publication is designed to provide accurate and personal experience information in regard to the subject matter covered. It is sold with the understanding that the author, contributors, publisher are not engaged in rendering counseling or other professional services. If counseling advice or other expert assistance is required, the services of a competent professional person should be sought out.

Good-bye To My Favourite Aunt

Myrna Seagrave

Dedication

To all especially the children who may need encouragement to tell their story.

To Gillie Rowland (Gillie E. J. Bolton) who inspired me to write this manuscript. Debbie Hiscock for her part in editing. Finding words like enervative instead of innovated. Last but not least Caroline Le Roux.

Prologue

I wanted to say something, at the beginning of this book which was intelligent, equal to Gillie Rowland who so kindly helped me start this journey many years ago. In 1985, I joined an Adult Literacy Long Distance Learning Programme. I felt very inadequate and no matter what I said I could never equal her writing, her knowledge of the English language being far superior. Though at one point, it had become almost as if I have left a task half done; I had to look at it like doing the laundry; until the ironing is done the laundry is an unfinished job; how I hate a job half done! So this introduction has to be attempted: I do think if I was to be able to get Gillie to participate in the publishing of this book it would serve not only as a book to read but a great educational tool to many teachers and scholars alike.

I do agree with everything which has been said and written as part of her assistance with this book. That, I feel only comes from the complete trust and confidence which arises from working so closely with one's teacher. Do we not, as small children, trust our parents completely? Understanding their motives only comes much later, if it materialises at all. When I see the individual words which Gillie has used I think; well they are no more grand or sophisticated than some of those that I have used at times. Then you look deeper into it: the sentence structure is more complex, the entire mechanics of her writing is different. This doesn't cause me concern, I just accept that fact, admitting I don't understand it, just as I could not understand a workshop manual. There was a period when I would regard myself as just being 'thick'. I now appreciate that that's not the case; it is just not my field of study, just as the mechanics of the English language is not my field. Why one writes in a particular manner and not in another is unknown to me, I am not that clever.

My book was something which has been stored for many years. The episodes had no complexities to them. They are just one event after another and that's how they are written. I once thought no wonderful lessons were learned in my childhood. I now know that every lesson which I learnt was wonderful. To understand the complexities of each event, Gillie has tapped into the depths of my writing and come up with some of the folds which occurred, much like the earth's movement, folding and sinking to produce the scenery, the end product.

I have a slight feeling of guilt, producing what all who have read my work say is excellent. If that is the case, why am I taking up someone's time and resources? Why didn't I pass English O Level? I hope that those who read it see beyond the mere words on the page. Those words were, at times, very difficult to find, some took as long as two hours. Words which I had no mental picture of their structure, but felt sure I had seen them in a book, read and reread the books, scanning the pages for my one word. Now in Australia, having access to the Internet, life is so much easier; even the worst combination of a word, Google will find it and set you right.

My book as it unfolded was in many ways therapeutic; as a way of helping me understand the many horrors of my childhood and because of this I have left none of them out. I asked a very good, dear, honest, and forthright friend to read this manuscript in 2010 and his advice to me was, "Take out the references to the sordid and perverted behaviour of some individuals (almost every family has the bastards lurking in the proverbial cupboard)" That is so true, he did lurk in the cupboard from the people looking in no one ever knew what hell we as kids and my mother were going through. I did give his opinion some serious thought but then I thought, "what was it that I want to achieve by writing down an account of my childhood which has had such a profound effect on me and my life way into adulthood?" To take any episode out gives people licence to think while this happens behind closed doors it is OK. I think taking out any section sends the wrong message. As children, we were always told by both Adam and my mother, "what happened at home stayed at home." This statement has had a very lasting and profound effect on every one of us kids; it sent the message that no matter what, there was no one who would protect or help us; it told us that we had to fight every battle on our own; something each of us has tried to do all through our adulthood.

Some of the siblings still refuse to ask for help. I am going to leave every word in. This I hope will make it more difficult for people like Adam; they ought never to be able to hide in the cupboard because children are too afraid to speak out. This was a very difficult journey for me, but if it gives other children the courage to speak out, it has served at least one purpose. At different times, I have asked myself why at this stage did I need help? Perhaps all I lack is self confidence, or maybe I have always had so much to say and no one has ever had the time to listen; the only way to make them listen is to write it down.

I can only conclude my introduction with a short statement. Thanks, Gillie, it would be fantastic if just one other person learns as much, from my efforts, as I have done. Good luck to all who try.

Myrna Seagrave

> LOOIJ—To Sylvia (Nee Benadie) and Marinis of Salisbury, on the 28 April 1953, at the Lady Chancellor Maternity Hospital, a daughter and little sister for Floris William. Thanks to Doctors and Staff.

My mother, as indeed all mothers perhaps do, had a romantic dream. Her daughter was going to climb high mountains and gain fame and success. Then she took a second look and had second thoughts. I did not look like a mountaineer, perhaps something a little more down-to-earth but definitely off the ground. That is it, the stage! Her idol at the time was Shirley Temple but that did not fit in with my surname, (I was also to find out much later that it was thanks to my Dad for my name) the next best was Myrna Loy. I was christened Myrna Elizabeth Looij.

My parents divorced in 1954 while living in Wankie. Unlike my father, my mother remarried, and we lost contact with our natural father. My mother, Willy, 3, and me, a year old, moved to Bulawayo to live with my grandmother, Ouma Benadie

Adam Theron, our stepfather had also been married before, his daughter Betty lived with his parents. Betty, after spending a short stay with us as a family, decided that she was far more fortunate to be with her grandparents. Betty had never truly known her father; Adam had had no contact with her since he left her with his parents at ten months old. She was legally adopted in 1966 by Ouma and Oupa Theron.

Our family began to increase in 1961 with the arrival of Gretha, then Petronella (28 June 1962-12 November 2013), and Ockert in 1963. My mother was very ill after Ockert was born and with each baby her eyesight worsened. She was advised not to have any more children.

We had a very extensive itinerary beginning in 1959 when we left Bulawayo to live in Wankie. We returned to Bulawayo in 1961. Bulawayo was our home for a brief six months. Towards Christmas of that year we moved to Ndola in Zambia. Before June 1963, we returned to Bulawayo. In 1965, we made our way to Chiredzi where we lived, until late 1968, when our family began to drift their separate ways. During my twelve years at school, I attended eleven different schools, nine being in the first part of my schooling from the age of 6 to 12.

Willy and I differ on the reason why we moved so much. My thoughts are that my stepfather was a mere rolling stone and also because he worked for a number of years with the Rhodesia Railways. Willy has a more sinister view. Willy went to South Africa when I went to live in the Rhodesian Childrens Home, in Salisbury. After a short separation from each other, Adam, my mother, and the other three siblings, continued their travels.

I completed my schooling in November 1971 and joined the staff at Salisbury Central Hospital.

In 1972, on 6 June, Keith and I were married. Our first son, Mark, was born on Friday, 13 April 1973. After spending a brief time at Alaska Mine in Sinoia, we returned to Salisbury where Allan was born on Thursday, 23 May 1975.

In 1979, December 12, we left Rhodesia behind to immigrate to Britain. I felt I had lost something very dear to me. I have now come to regard Rhodesia as a favourite aunt of mine, who died that sad day. This way, I am able, in my own mind, to justify leaving behind something I love so deeply.

A number of people have written about Rhodesia, and in most of these books, one is given, however slight, a glimpse into the political drama.

I have tried to stay away from the political side of our country and chosen my words carefully, refraining from words which have political connotations. My story is simple, about people living together, each playing their part in society. Like elsewhere, people have a part to play in their country, Rhodesia has normal people, living normal lives. I write about our ordinary way of life, drawing the attention of the reader to what I take for fact, including the beauty of the country and the people. One day, someone cleverer than myself will tell the Rhodesian's story more fully. We, the people, have a place of importance in whichever country we happen to live.

Wankie

I was one year old, in 1954, when my mother and father separated. For me, their divorce had no significance, and until I was fourteen years old, my father was just a name. Willy and I lived with Ouma Benadie, my mother's mother, in Queens Park West in Bulawayo.

My mother worked away from home and only came home for weekends. Then one day, there was this man. Never before had we seen Mommy with anyone. My mother and Adam were married on February 29, 1959. When they were married, my mother stopped working and we all lived together. It was not long after, when we moved from Ouma Benadie's house, to stay with Adam's friends, that I started school. This was where my life started to take shape.

My mother walked me down to Newmansford School in Queens Park West, on my first day at school. Very much like my son, I disregarded my mother's fussing and took my seat. I was so proud; I was, after all, a big girl now. I went to 'Big School.' Some children cried and kicked. I stood in absolute bewilderment, not understanding what all the fuss was about. Once the parents had left, we were all seated on the floor. We were to have a story.

The teacher sat on a chair. Still today, this image is firmly imprinted in my mind. Though now, when I think about it, it really must be my imagination. Never was the teacher's chair that high. We children all sat on the floor looking up to this very, very high person. My hair seemed to be anchored to my back pulling my head upwards. The story, I have no memory of, but should have liked it to have been Aesop's Fables. Something distracted my attention and I noticed this small trickle. "Oh no! I have wet my pants." I started to fidget. The teacher was quick, she noticed my predicament. I remember so clearly. "Never mind, Myrna," she said, "but next time you must ask to go to the toilet." With that, I started to cry. The floor was cleaned for me, and my pants were taken and washed. At the end of the day, when they were dry, I got them back. I had been at Newmansford School for a term. Adam was a shunter on the Rhodesia Railways. The railway network in both the Federation Countries and Bechuanaland Protectorate (Botswana), were owned by the Rhodesia Railways. As part of their contract, all employees were, if necessary, transferred between these countries. Our travels began around May of the same year. Travelling from place to place had the advantage of meeting many different people and seeing numerous places. It brings to mind a little boy. He lived in the Rhodesian Children's Home. He maintained he was a very lucky boy as he had two mommies and two daddies. I too must have been very fortunate, travelling the length and breadth of Rhodesia. The many people I came into contact with have truly helped to shape my life. It would not have the interest which it has had.

Wankie is situated some three hundred miles from Bulawayo in a North Westerly direction; this was where our first home was to be as a new family. Though I had lived in Wankie before, the only period I remember is my second stay, from May 1959 until 1961.

Shortly after arriving in Wankie, it was decided that Willy's health would improve if he had his tonsils out. Like the fashion world, the medical profession has phases and it was during one of these phases, it was said that I too should have mine out. We would be able to keep each other company and besides which my tonsils were of no use to me. Our beds were booked, we had a little side ward. As Willy was the eldest, it was arranged he would go first. A short time after Willy was collected by the nuns, the same nuns fetched me. Just before going into the theatre, I noticed Willy just outside of the theatre door on his hard, cold stainless steel trolley, still wide awake.

The next time I saw Willy, we were back in our ward. My mother was standing next to Willy. He had not woken up yet. He also had a large gas bottle next to his bed and a plastic see-through tent over him. Willy, nine years old, had fought against the anaesthetic and refused to go to sleep. That night I was eating jelly and ice cream and Willy was still asleep. I can remember asking why Willy was not awake but other than that, I had little concern as to when he would wake up.

The next day, waking up, Willy was out of his tent but a mask and gas bottle remained at his bed. It was only when I was a lot older, in my first year as a student nurse, that the incident was fully explained to me. Then I recalled Willy had asked me how many numbers I had counted up to and him bragging that he had got up to twenty or thirty. Willy had asked if he could be awake while they took his tonsils out and the doctor told him that he had to go to sleep. This was the first time Willy displayed how strong a will power he had. Not being able to give him a larger dose he was pushed into the corridor where, hopefully, he would drop off to sleep. Willy was in fact given a stronger drug. He then developed breathing problems.

Wankie was always very hot and it only ever rained once while we lived there, some two and a half years. So as to contain the dust most people laid granite stones along their driveways. We, on the other hand, always used what was freely available, and if not then usually the cheapest. We had our driveway laid out with coal cinders called coke by the locals. The little narrow footpath from the small gate was lined with these cinders and edged with white lime wash painted stones.

Willy and I both went home together, but Willy still looked very thin and pale. My mother, attention being mainly on Willy, never noticed my slight limp a few weeks after coming home. Then one day my foot was very sore and my limp very pronounced. My mother looked at it and said that I had something in it and that it had gone septic. While Adam held me, my mother dug it out. Screaming with the pain, I started to choke. My stepfather let me go, my mother thumped my back, and at the sight of the large dark red lump of what looked like liver, I stopped short.

My mother, seizing her opportunity, grabbed my foot and gave one firm squeeze and out came a small piece of coke. "Ouch!" was about as much as I dared say—thinking that I had screamed my liver up a moment before. Still looking in bewilderment at my hand, my mum showed me the coke. I asked her "what should I do with this," showing her my hand. She said it was only a clot of blood and to throw it away. Feeling slightly deflated at the thought that it was not my liver, I threw it away.

The school which both my brother and I went to was in the main town centre of Wankie which was some distance away. Adam's firm lay on a bus. The bus stop was quite a little way away from the house and we had then to walk down thirty nine steps. Going down was fun—we would just straddle, tummy down, over the two and a half inch water pipe banister. The older children started off right at the top, but not being so brave, the little ones only managed the last few steps and even then we had to be caught at the bottom. Starting off at the top was something each of us aspired to and measured our growth against; much like my own children measured themselves against reaching the light switch without having to stand on a chair.

The heat was so intense that the school started a lot earlier and finished at twelve o'clock. Even this sometimes was not good enough. Often, climbing up our mountain of steps, I would take a lot of coaxing. My brother, more often than not, weighted down with his own books, would have to carry mine. One of his games that did not catch on was "I will race you to the top." Once he got two steps in front of me, I would just sit down and cry, refusing to move. When he was in a good mood, he would pretend it was a mountain and we were famous, climbing Mount Everest.

Wankie consists of the main township and three collieries, appropriately called numbers One, Two, and Three. All three mines are shaft mines with huge, gigantic black hills around them. These large slag dumps had small burning pockets in them and on a dark night, sitting in the cool of the evening, one was able to see them glowing red. It was seeing this red glow on the horizon, perhaps, that reminded my mother of a tale she was told as a child (I say tale because I am not in a position to say with absolute certainty that it was true. I have found references to a much later event *(Zimbabwe (Rhodesia) 6 June 1972 Wankie coal mine disaster Methane explosion. One of the worst mining disasters with 426 fatalities)*. Provided by an article "Mining: Friend or Foe"? Economic, Environmental & Social Impacts—an Overview written by Golam Kibria Ph.D; March 2013 *(ResearchGate Community Support 5idzs@support.researchgate.net)*

Being unguarded, by either a fence or barrier, the children played on them. Not seeing the danger, one little girl fell into just such a pocket and paid dearly for playing so close to a furnace. By some miracle, she was pulled out. With the intense heat, her arm and leg muscles had constricted as though she had received a severe electric shock. The area that caused the most concern was her throat; her chin was moulded on to the uppermost part of her chest. There was fear that the cartilage rings making up the trachea were damaged. Rhodesia not having, at that time, facilities to deal with such extensive burns had the child sent to South Africa. The backs of her calves were surgically removed from her thighs and just as skilfully were her arms separated. She was able to have plastic surgery on her throat and chest. Further to the tale, the Rhodesian State Lotteries financed a greater part of the bill. The slag dumps never held any fascination for us. Whether it was because of the tale, in which case it served a purpose, or perhaps it was because we were not miners' children.

Why we moved houses, I don't know, or indeed the time we moved, but our next house was off the hill and much older. At one time, our second house was on stilts. At a later date, the portion between the ground and the floor of the house was boarded up with a few steps leading up to the veranda which surrounded all four sides of the house. Very vaguely I can remember only once going into the dark cave through a trap door in the floor to look for something. This experience is almost like trying to recall a dream so maybe that's what it was. The floor however was made up of four inch wide planks, and in some places, the knots in the wood had shrunk and fallen out. Not having a carpet, we did lose little things like rubbers and pencils. Sometimes for devilment, I can remember pushing teaspoons down these holes. Under the house, the soft damp earth was cool and the spiders made their webs freely. When the sun had sunk very low and the moon was beginning to rise, the spiders, large, long-legged, orange-red, hunting spiders would emerge. Their eyesight being very poor they would chase any shadow, very often it was our shadows.

Adam hated these spiders and yet he always seemed to encounter sometimes as many as three at once. We were all sitting on the bottom step, barefoot as usual, when Adam sitting some distance away, on a large boulder, leapt up into the air and came prancing towards the veranda as though the devil himself was after him. At the same time, one would have thought he was walking on eggs as no sooner had one foot touched the ground when it was up in the air again. Swearing, was not uncommon for Adam; his mother tongue being Afrikaans he shouted "die vokking verdomde jaags spinnerkop" (the fucking damn randy spider) was after him again. He looked so comical. When reading different fairy tales of court jesters to my sons, Adam's figure springs to mind.

Although we seldom had enough money to go around, we always managed to have pets of some sort, mainly dogs, but while in our new house my mother had a budgerigar. Peter-boy was a pretty blue bird. We also had a cat, though I can't really remember ever having another one after Sammy. Peter, as we called him for short, was Sammy's best friend. Almost as if Peter could not fly, Sammy strutted round the house like a queen with Peter sitting on her head like a jewelled tiara. Adam had taught Peter to swear and when Adam lolled home in his drunken stupor, Peter, sitting on the centre lampshade, called him every name under the sun. Adam's drunken state was as regular as clock work; every night when the lights were turned out Peter would take his pew. We sometimes thought Adam did this nightly ritual just to please Peter. He took much delight in relaying to all he met how his wife's bird swore at him for coming home drunk.

The housing estates in Wankie, except for those in the main township, were not very extensive and many homes backed on to empty wasteland. The grass stood dry and brittle, like sticks of macaroni. Veld fires were very common, most of the time they were started deliberately. It was the only way to keep the snake population down and out of one's home. A fire was also a solution for the rotting carcasses. The stench was often overpowering, though we never had any encounter with anything larger than a 'Meerkat' (a true Meerkat is of the weasel family but we called feral cats Meerkats). One evening while my parents were at the country club, Willy and I were drying the dishes. All the outside doors were open and so naturally were the inter-leading doors, we had just not got round to closing them; the evening cool was as welcome as a cold shower. Willy spotted him first, my back was to the dining room; "There's a Meerkat in the house", he shouted. We both had the same thought at once—Sammy's tiara. We ran shouting and stamping our feet loudly on the wooden floor waving the tea towels wildly. We were too late. Peter gave one last 'Chirp'. The Meerkat broadsided round the table legs as he ran for cover through the door and into the dark. Peter's blue-grey feathers settled on the floor. Willy, obsessed with getting even with the cat, chased him out of the house. Even as the cat disappeared with the bird still in his mouth, Willy pelted it with stones. Willy was more aware of the trouble we were in than I. He waited up till our parents came home to tell my mother what had happened to her bird. My mother told Adam in the morning, when he enquired why Peter had not greeted him, that Peter had died of old age.

Happier days, we spent at the Victoria Falls. In every book that has been written about Rhodesia, one will always read of the splendour and magnitude of these falls. It is a sight that has a different appeal to all that see it, and although it is not one of the Seven Wonders of the World, it does stir one's emotions.

I did, at one time, think that the present government would change its name back to what it was originally known as before David Livingstone renamed it Victoria Falls. Mosi-oa—Tunya, which means "the smoke that thunders." During the rainy season when two hundred and forty million cubic gallons of water plunges over its ledge the white spray clouds can be seen for sixty miles.

When we visited the Victoria Falls some years ago there were no fences or restriction barriers, just small discreet notices advising you not to venture beyond that point. Even the historic baobab tree near Devil's Cataract was not fenced off. This tree served as a landmark in the earlier Pioneer days. The tree is reputed to be two thousand years old and although it takes twelve men, arms stretched out, finger tips touching to encircle it; it is by no means the biggest of its kind.

The Falls and other historical places would not hold as much fascination as they do without little tales and legends that have passed down from one generation to another. One such tale is: The turmoil within the Boiling Pot is so great that when a railway line track was held in it the power of the water twisted and distorted it so that it resembled an oversized cork screw. The Boiling Pot to most looked like a cul-de-sac the water cascaded over the falls and rushed down to into the pot

Just before the bridge, on the Rhodesian side, is a large lay-by, many people park their cars and walk across the bridge often pausing in the middle to look at the Falls, in mid-air. It was while at this point my mother looked back at the car and seeing a few baboons milling round the cars and in the trees, she told us of her first visit to Victoria Falls. Willy was still a baby and I was not yet born. They had left the car as we had done that day, not suspecting the baboons. On their return, they found they had left the car windows open. Baboons are very destructive. They had ransacked the car ripping all the seat covers. Willy's napkins were in shreds and hanging on the trees like white festoon garlands. Baboons are not only very maternal but also clever. Mothers who had babies had fought over possession for Willy's clothes; one had in fact acquired a jersey. Another had found his bottle and was feeding her baby its contents. Grinning and chattering to herself, she sat on the ground in the shade of a tree.

The baboons still remain but not in such numbers, driven away by man. The tourist board had seen fit to remind travellers of their presence. Large posters saying "LOCK YOUR CARS SECURELY" were put up all along the road and in the lay-by. The baboons' only natural enemy, the leopard had also seen these partially tame animals as an easy meal.

My parents enjoyed being outdoors and when we were not out on a picnic they played jukskei (an adaptation of horse-shoe). It was not a very strenuous game and mostly played by the Afrikaans community.

While the adults played their game, we children either played in the adventure playground or made use of the swimming pool, if there was one. Jukskei consists of two large sand pits with a stump, very much like a cricket stump, in the middle. Each player has a set, two skeie. The skeies were originally made of wood. Though the design of a large necked bottle did not change, the wood was replaced by solid rubber. The object of the game was to get a score of twenty-one, by means of either hitting the stump clean out of the sand or landing as close to it as possible. Four points were for "Pen le," which meant that you hit the stump out of the sand but your skeie lay closest to it. All the skeie were weighted and the women, being considered the weaker of the sexes, usually took the lighter ones, throwing from the closest line to the opposite sand pit. The men, with the heavier skeie, throw from a line behind the ladies. Once the whole team had thrown, the score was counted and the whole process started again continuing on with the score. If, however, you achieved more than twenty-one in any session you had to start from nothing again. This was one game that we played at home; visiting friends were roped in to make up the teams. The evening was rounded off with a braai-vleis (barbecue). When the sand pits were not in use, seeing as they were filled with clean river sand, they made excellent children's sand pits; the drawback was as more people moved into the area and brought their cats they became an ideal sand box.

Bulawayo

Willy's health was not improving, and my mother too began to look ill. Adam, being on the Rhodesian Railways, asked for a transfer, and in 1961, we moved back to Bulawayo and set down roots once again. We lived in Westgate which is a suburb of Bulawayo.

Bulawayo was considered to have a healthier climate than Wankie. Wankie lies in a depression. Although it is no longer within the Tsetse Fly belt, the Anopheles Mosquitoes have not been eradicated. The older folk maintain that because it hardly ever rained in Wankie the different diseases were never washed away. Bulawayo has a higher rainfall than Wankie and is situated on the plateau which runs through the middle of Rhodesia. The temperature therefore is not so severe. My mother's growth, which is what a Wankie doctor diagnosed, was given a second opinion when we arrived in Bulawayo. Gretha was born on the 17 June 1961. Gretha was a responsibility that I enjoyed though Willy regarded her as just an addition to the family. Nevertheless this bright blue-eyed, blonde-haired baby took her place in the family.

While living in Westgate, we lived in two separate houses though we still went to the same school. The first house was a fair way from the school and as we never had the use of a bus perhaps that is why we moved to our second house. The very tall 'rubber hedge' of our back garden formed the fence with the school. Many houses, especially in the Bulawayo area, had rubber hedges planted round their boundary. It was always green, requiring no water, ever, other than when it rained.

The plant had no leaves, as such, but like the prickly pear cactus, it grew very thick. We all called it a rubber hedge but the white milky substance had no commercial value at all. In fact, it was a menace. The branches were difficult to break, almost bending back on themselves, secreting small drops of milk through their pores. The milk soon turned thick and sticky. If you got it into your eyes, they became very painful.

Just in front of this hedge was our Nannie's khaya. Miriam had her mother to stay for a short while, she was fascinating. All African women, at one time, wore a doek (Afrikaans for scarf) covering their head entirely. When I asked Miriam why she wore a doek all the time, she said it was not right for a young woman not to wear one. This idea has changed and now only the older Africans still wear a doek outside of her own home. The doek as I knew it has been replaced by the very fashionable statement headwear being worn by many African women. As a doek was the norm in the 60s, An African woman smoking was very much a rarity. Miriam's mother, not only did she not wear a doek but she also smoked a pipe! I would often be found sitting cross-legged in front of this very grey-haired lady, mesmerised by the smoke like signals whirling out of her pipe.

The old woman sat, most days on a grass mat, very straight and without a back support. Only when she sat on an old kitchen chair round the front of the khaya did she cover her head. Once he found out that she could speak Swahili, Adam talked quite freely with her. This, she thought was marvellous; he as a White man could talk to her in her own language. Adam spoke seven African languages. During his episodes of doing the right thing, he was very sought after by church missionaries as their interpreter. It would infuriate him if they were an African and they could not talk their mother tongue after he had asked where they came from and he spoke to them in the appropriate language. Miriam could not speak Swahili because she grew up in South Africa. Her mother talked to her in Afrikaans. Miriam worked for us for a few months. Then one day, she said her mother was dying, and she wanted to go home. Adam said that he did not think that the old woman was her true mother but her grandmother as she was very old. This is possible. When an African woman has a child, very often if her circumstances don't allow her to leave work and look after the child, she in turn sends the child home to her mother. The grandmother, drinks herbs or even goes and sees a witchdoctor to bring her milk on. Then she is able to feed the baby. African children are breast fed until they are two or three years old.

We were all sad when Miriam took her mother home as when she left she said she would not come back to Rhodesia. She was going to stay in South Africa with her mother. I found this part confusing, looking back on it, as when I read up which part of South Africa spoke Swahili, found to my amazement that the origins of this language was Zanzibar. When I read on, I discovered that this small island was subjected to slave trades as were many parts in Africa. Some of these Africans found their way into missions and were used by the early missionaries, thus finding themselves in countries like South Africa.

A typical human trait to get us through all sad times is we reflect on the happy times and bring them to the fore ground. Miriam had all her boxes and suitcases and was walking down to the station. Adam said to her that she had better not use the bath on the train as it might have a barbel in it. A thin smile began to grow on her face until at last she could no longer balance the things on her head.

We had all been out fishing one Sunday and Uncle Harry had caught a barbel. Adam, knowing that Miriam enjoyed barbel, had brought it home for her. Miriam was not at home when we arrived; we filled the bath with water and put it in. This barbel was about two feet long. Miriam had come to work the next morning and seeing the bath full of water, the water was a little muddy too, just pulled the plug out. To her absolute horror the fish started flapping in the bath, trying, to swim upstream like a spawning salmon. Miriam let out an almighty scream as the fish jumped out of the bath. We all arrived in the bathroom. Miriam had fainted and the barbel was flapping helplessly on the floor.

After Miriam's departure, we left Westgate. Adam was once more transferred. We were off to Zambia——Ndola. Zambia lies to the North of Rhodesia and at the time, 1961, was still known as Northern Rhodesia. We lived with Auntie Muriel while my mother and Adam went to Ndola. There was, at the time, some doubt as to the size of the accommodation which was available in Zambia. Auntie Muriel, my mother's sister, and Uncle Harry, lived in Queens Park East. Although we were not able to still go to the same school, whilst living with Auntie Muriel, we did see the year out in a Rhodesian school.

Three months passed. I don't remember asking to be with my parents. I cried a little, when my mom's dog died. She missed my mom so much that she would not eat and lay in the road and refused to move. Sometimes, when Willy and I came home from school she came to meet Willy, but then after a short time, even Willy could not raise within her the will to move out of the road. One day, a car came round the corner too fast and saw her too late. The accident happened within days of my mother collecting Willy and I.

We arrived in Ndola just before Christmas 1961. Only two things stand out in my mind, well, maybe three. The first thing is huge red white ant hills (Termite mounds). All the soil was red in Ndola. We, as our luck would have it, arrived in the middle of the rainy season. What fun! The best slide that has ever to be discovered is one made from red mud and water. Groping on the branches and the smallest of weeds we pulled ourselves up the ant hill. Once at the top, we sat on our backsides and down we slithered. Sometimes we went so fast we landed up in a tangled mass at the bottom. Undeterred by our state, or anything, back up we went, till we could no more. Our feet felt like the lead weighted shoes of a diver, the mud was sometimes as thick as four inches on them. The proof of the number of times we had been down the hill was judged by the thickness of the mud on our soles. Eventually we could no longer lift our feet which now resembled a diver's footwear. With great pride we scraped the mud off with an ice-lolly stick, stacking it neatly on the side—there was lasting proof! Not that we needed any. Our plastered red bodies were proof enough. Before Adam came home, we had to wash ourselves outside with a hose pipe and our clothes went into a bucket of water, just for a rinse. On to the washing line then on again the next time for the slide of your life! Occasionally, we would notice the white ants repair the damage that we had done to their home but we never felt any guilt and it certainly never stopped us. Even when we felt that the rain was taking their side by not raining, well, out came the hose pipe and down we would go. Those days were not as good as when we played in the rain. We never met with any serious resistance from my mother. The only thing was that we had to wash our own clothes. Even now when watching the English version of "It's a Knock Out", the over dressed figures trying to walk up the slippery obstacles makes me quite beside myself. I imagine those small flimsy branches just out of their reach, as so often they were for me.

Every garden, without exception, had at least two mango trees in it. These were the most delicious mangos I have ever tasted. The trees, sturdy and as large as old apple trees, were ideal for climbing. Our fruit was never allowed to get too ripe. Like vultures, we would watch the small pea size green mango grow till it could eventually fit into a large man's hand. Still grass green and hard, we started to pick them. Once we, Willy and I, had finished off our fruit, we would start on someone else's fruit. There were always many people willing to give you their surplus. People always said the best place to eat a mango is in the bath. I had no such problems. There are two varieties. One is much smaller than the other and elongated, ripening with a yellow-red skin. The other, which is the type that grew in Ndola, were the Kidney Mangos. I had never seen them change colour, but they did get soft.

The flesh is bright yellow and has a fibrous texture. They have a fairly large pip, and unless one has a firm hold of it, it slips out of one's hand and all you have left is the thick yellow juice running down between the backs of your fingers. A toothpick is often needed to dislodge the hairs from between one's teeth. Unlike an orange, where one can taste the sharp acetic acid, a mango is not sharp but it does contain a high concentration of acetic acid which, if left round your mouth, will in fact burn you. The after effects were known as Mango Sores.

The other incident that happened was mainly to do with Gretha. The first house that we lived in only had two bedrooms. As Gretha was only a few months old, she slept in my mother's bedroom. In the very early hours of one morning, Gretha woke up crying. This was most unusual. My mother got up to see to her. She thanked Adam for lighting a match but said that she could see. Adam's reply was that he was holding no match. With that, a black hand withdrew from the window dropping the burning cloth into the bedroom. Adam flew out of the bed, out of the front door, chasing the African. The only problem was that Adam never slept with a stitch of clothing whatsoever. He got to the gate, some fifty yards away from the front door. He then realised his state and crept back into the house like a cat burglar in the pantomimes looking over his shoulder with every step.

Meanwhile, my mother had put out the small fire in the bedroom. We 'phoned the police who came round and explained the idea of a burning rag. The African had no intention of burning the house down but the cloth was impregnated with paraffin, the burning fumes from which induce a very heavy sleep. Having done this, they would have been able to walk out with the contents of our whole house, even the beds on which we slept. The police explained that they were a very well organised gang who had vans waiting at the ready to take the items away. We moved from that house shortly afterwards and were given a larger house with a larger garden. It had two ant hills and four Mango trees.

Many of the older folk said that Gretha was psychic. I should not like to comment but certainly Gretha is able to do and say some strange things. One incident comes to mind immediately. Gretha was three years old, and woke up at half past five during the week. She was crying, there was, she said, a man in the garden. As it was just getting light Adam took her outside. There was no one there, yet as they stood in front of the Mulberry tree Gretha insisted that this man was there.

The household was already awake. They thought no more of it and Adam went off to work. Later that morning he telephoned my mother to say the man who worked with him and to whom he gave a lift every day had died at half past five that morning.

These peculiar happenings became fewer and fewer as Gretha grew older. Gretha remains a very cautious person and superstitious in the extreme.

We left Ndola after Adam was fired from the Rhodesian Railways; he hit another member of staff at work and we were told to leave Zambia within 24 hours. A few months before Petronella's birth on the 28 June 1963, we were back in Rhodesia. Adam was still out of work. We had arrived with little or no furniture and only the things we were able to move with us in the car. Adam and my mother went to Social Welfare for assistance. The result for us was because Adam was fired he had to sell his car and anything other than what the government of the day felt was an absolute necessity; the welfare calculated what Adam would be able to get for his car; his payout, and any other items the money should last our family for a preset time. We were sent away and told to come back when the money had run out. Salaries were paid monthly and I can remember that Adam and Willy went into town and had to be at the local municipal markets before the general public were allowed to compete for the goods sold; the market opened at 5.30 a.m. to the general public. Items which were considered absolutely necessary were a fridge as Gretha was only just over a year and Petronella was a newborn; she was not breast fed. A TV was not considered essential as was a cooker; one could make a fire outside and cook on that! Ouma Mollentze was the head cook at the local mental institution known at the time as the Ingutsheni would start work at 4 a.m. and so Adam was able to get a lift into town where we had been given coupons so that we could purchase food, vegetables, and meat. He would push the day's purchase in the pram home. We stayed with Auntie Muriel and Uncle Harry's mother, Ouma Mollentze she had a plot in Kingsdale (that is one difficult concept for most to come to terms with growing up and especially the Afrikaans people, either everyone was; Auntie, Uncle or Ouma and Oupa depending on the age gap even if they are no relation to you whatsoever. It does become very confusing). Adam managed to gain employment at a bakery while we lived with Ouma Mollentze.

The bakery, at which he worked, started at 6 p.m. and carried on till eleven o'clock. Adam often brought home piping hot doughnuts. While they were still warm, we all had a midnight feast of doughnuts and tea. My love for doughnuts was forged there, but much like a drug addict trying to replicate that first perfect high, I am still looking for that one perfect doughnut as I remember them.

Willy, being thirteen, went to Northlea High School. Leaving early in the morning, he had to cycle thirteen miles to school. The Northlea Pipe Band could be heard on practice days. Northlea in Bulawayo and Churchill Boys' High in Salisbury are the only two schools in Rhodesia who have a pipe band. Year after year, the contest goes on between the two schools and is taken very seriously, much like the Oxford and Cambridge Boat Race.

I went to the nearest school which was Kingsdale. I spent only a term there but have two wonderful memories. The school was only small, having three classrooms. The playground provided the main attraction, it had a Maypole. Unlike the brightly coloured ribboned ones on picture cards, ours had short and long fat twisted grey aging rope. Some lengths had huge untidy knots tied at the ends, while others still had the wooden bars plaited into their ends. The wood shone brightly, having been highly polished with many sweaty hands. It was the race any Olympian would be proud to have been a part of to get to the maypole first; each rope had an excited child hanging off it and then the fun began. Round we would run until the speed of the group lifted your legs off the ground. Squeals of excitement replaced the silence of the classrooms.

The other memory, the best one of all, was my trip to the seaside. One day, some people came to the school and every child was asked to fill in a questionnaire. The two main questions were; had we ever had a holiday out of Rhodesia? The other, had we ever had a holiday at the seaside?

Some time later, my parents received a letter saying that I had been picked to go to the seaside, all the way down to Simonstown in Cape Town, South Africa. This is a holiday that the Social Welfare undertook each year for a large number of children throughout Rhodesia. During the Second World War, my mother went on one as well but as the war restricted traffic between the different countries, her team went to

The Vumba in the North Eastern Highlands of Rhodesia. The holiday is funded, completely, by charity and the government; the only thing you are asked to provide is the pocket money. My parents were not in a position to give me the required twenty pounds so Ouma Molletze gave me the money.

Leaving Rhodesia, we travelled by train through Botswana down to Cape Town. From Cape Town Central station we went by an electric train to Simonstown. From that station we went by coach to the boarding hostel. The hostel has its own private beach but we were also able to use the Seaforth Beach which was a public beach.

One afternoon, some people came, they were all in black wet suits and they were diving around the rocks, on which was built a restaurant. The story was that someone had come across an octopus nestled in the rocks. The men said they were from the Stellenbosch University and were going to take it away. Deep down I was very pleased when the end of the day came and they had not found him.

While we were there once the tide came in. It lived up to its name 'The Cape of Storms'. The wind whipped up the waves so high their peaks had white beards on them from a distance the larger ones looked like snow covered mountain peaks as the white water rushed to the bottom of the slop and disappeared into the vast ocean. It washed all sorts of strange things up on to the beach. I found a sailor's button and also a small squid-like thing. No one knew quite what it was.

To keep these high tides contained, a wall some twenty foot high was built with steps going down to the beach. Above the wall were beautiful lawns and large shady palms and flamboyant trees. The beach was not very wide but was very, very long. Most of our two weeks were spent playing in the sand and swimming. The hostel gave us a good breakfast, and we always had a packed lunch, returning in the evening for our supper.

Sometime during our stay, members of the Cape Town Round Table came and we all had a day out. We were all divided up into small groups of four or five depending on the size of our host's car. Some went to Table Mountain while our party and others went to Stellenbosch Zoo. I was sad; thinking of the vast ocean the octopus had to swim in and perhaps if he had been caught, he too would find his way into a small cage like the leopard. The only animals that I really enjoyed were the little wild hares that were hopping around quite freely. They were quite tame, coming to you for tid-bits. The little red tree squirrels were not quite so tame but did collect the food if you left it on the grass.

My holiday was soon at an end and back into Cape Town we went. On our return journey, we passed through the Kalahari Desert during the day. It was very hot. The water in the glass bottles was very warm and not pleasant to drink. Our engine was a 'puffing Billy' the older steam engines were still in abundance in Rhodesia. In 1963, there were only a few diesel engines. This did not help matters as the soot drifted in through all the open windows. Air conditioned trains were unheard of in Rhodesia.

As a present for my mother, I had brought a jar of seawater home with a small piece of brown, twisting, slimy seaweed. We had been on the train for four days and four nights, and the water didn't smell very nice. While holding the jar of water it was very difficult to explain how lovely it was to swim in the sea, better than any river or canal.

Until this holiday, and ever since, that is until I left home, our family went to Ouma and Oupa Theron for our holidays. Adam's parents farmed and managed a number of farms, all of which were tobacco farms. I think we must have stayed at all of them at one time or another. We returned yearly for our Christmas school holidays. The holidays spent at Eenheid (Oneness) are the most memorable. Christmas at the farm was, to all of us, like rainwater in a tired fish tank.

Where we were living seemed to be of little consequence. Oupa's farms were mainly to the north east of the capital, Salisbury. Though once he did farm in Eiffel Flats between Gatooma and Hartley. This area is mainly suited to cotton, the soil being heavy black clay. During this particular period, cotton was not grown widely and the tobacco crops brought in a higher price.

To accommodate us, the community, the school holidays were broken into three weeks at Easter, three weeks in August and six weeks at Christmas. This gradually changed 'til in 1969 the school term consisted of three, four-week holidays and a working term of about two months.

Eenheid is between Mrewa and Macheke but closer to Macheke which is some eighty miles east of Salisbury. Our furthest journey was from Chiredzi to Macheke, though it was nearly four hundred miles, the journey was always completed in one day. The roads were very good with many picturesque lay-bys. These always had a large shady tree. The table came with its own 'ant-table cloth', after all no picnic is complete without little black ants and flies. We, like many I should think, had our favourite lay-bys and although we always tried to stop at the same one, if someone else had already stopped there, depending on the size, we nearly always moved on. Disappointed cries of, "Ah, they are at our lay-by," came from the back seats. Our very best lay-by was just outside of Marandellas towards Macheke. It was large enough for perhaps three cars, but there were only two tables underneath the shade of a huge Lucky Bean tree (Erythrina Abyssinica). The duration of our stop, between sandwiches and tea, was spent trying to find the reddest and biggest lucky bean, and always just a few feet away from the one already picked up was another just that little bit bigger or perhaps brighter. Our plastic bags full and the stop at an end, we would have to return to the car.

The lucky bean tree has a spectacular coral red flower which comes out before the leaves. The flower dies leaving small pea pods, constricted between seeds, hanging like drying strips of meat in the new foliage. Although the tree is often large and sturdy, it is not easy to climb because of its thorny branches and rough thick pale corky bark. The best beans were on the ground. Some were bright red while others were more deep orange with a black spot and round or oval in shape, not unlike black eyed beans. Many beans would find their way into curio shops as necklaces. The soft bark was also used in the trade for carvings.

My mother would, for days afterwards, find lucky beans in the house and clothes and we were lucky if we did not have them thrown out; although this was not the reason for their name. The seeds do contain a large number of alkaloids that are known to be highly toxic, but it's said to be used in traditional medicine suggestions that they have antibacterial, anti-inflammatory and analgesic effects. The Africans said the seeds had a certain luck attached and were used as lucky charms.

After our last stop, we turned off the good tar road and made our way to the farm. All the windows open, the car left clouds of white dust in a turmoil as it sped along the dirt road. Some miles later, we sighted the first farm gate. This was flanked on either side of the road by stranded barbed wire fence—the boundary of Oupa's six thousand acre farm. A short time later, we came to the farm yard gate. Very tall old conifer trees flanked either side of the white sandy road. The road was narrow and the trees formed a canopy towering high above us, allowing the sun through in places as the breeze moved their branches gracefully, the sun only appeared in irregular light and dark patches on the road like an uneven patchwork quilt, unlike the daisies on the front lawn which were now in full view.

Daisy lawns were very popular at one time. I must say seeing the snow on the ground, the little white daisies look just as splendid. They were a constant source of nectar to the honey bee and made playing on it most uncomfortable.

Ouma, quiet and gentle, walked out on to the veranda, when the barking dogs drew her attention to our approach. Small and petite with her grey waist-long hair plaited, rolled and pinned into a bun, she stood her pride and joy surrounding her. The veranda surrounded three sides of the house cooling and darkening it, but it was the ideal place for her ferns, standing on four bricks in brightly coloured, halved forty-four gallon drums. The well-polished red cement floor was a striking contrast, reflecting the depth of drum and plant. Beautiful shades of green stood out against the white lime washed walls. The best fern of all was the watery green asparagus hanging over its drum, like an over sized bottle brush. My Ouma's favourite was the softer, brighter green Maidenhair fern. In a bottle green drum, the healthy dark straight leaves of the more common fern stood proud and tall.

Looking out on to the lawn, also in drums, shaded from the sun, were a splendid show of hydrangeas. A more spectacular show I have only seen growing in the wild at Vumba. From the common pink and blue to a deep, almost mauve-blue, like an enlarged pin cushion, the flowers protruded from the leaves. The one that fascinated me most was a white one. One half of the plant had bright white flowers and as though it were two plants, the other half had smaller pale watery green clusters.

The other side of the veranda was always in the shade and not many plants would thrive there so it was reserved for 'doppies.' Thank goodness for the tall Blue Gum Trees which were planted many years ago to hide the unsightly water tanks used for storing the house water pumped up from the river. We had one tank which collected the rain water off the farm roof which was connected to all the cold water taps in the house.

Doppies, (used cartridge cases) when played, were played on Sunday afternoons. After a really scrumptious lunch followed by a fresh plum or peach from the orchard, we would begin. To set up our game, one team would sit on their mats as close to the outer wall of the veranda as they could and the others were as close to the creamery, some fourteen or fifteen feet away. The doppies were empty .303 and .202 cartridge shells. So long as both teams had equal amounts, numbers were not important. The doppies were lined up on the floor in front of your mat, strategically, with one small doppie some distance in front, it had been painted either with a red or blue band, it was the general. A coin was tossed; the team that won fired the first of many cannon balls. The cannon ball was a fairly large goon' (metal ball bearing varying in size from a small marble to the largest one). Ours was about the size of a 50p piece. The goon was rolled between the two teams, each trying with whatever skill or luck they had to knock over the other team's doppies. The goon rolled loudly along the cement floor, some cracks working for you, others against. As the goon was rolling along the floor the odd flaw, could be picked up by the more hollow sound. Sometimes the goon had to be rolled at quite a speed to keep it straight, then it was wiser to use the mat, picked up like a tunnel, to catch it. On occasions the teams had to be made up by my mother but more often than not we would have visitors and there were enough to make up four or six aside.

During the week, when everyone was busy, we kids would have to make up our own games. One of these was rolling on a water drum. On the same side as our doppies veranda, between the big blue gum trees, was a water drum that had a leak in it. We would climb on to this with the help of a forty-four gallon drum and walk on it. We went slowly at first, and then as the drum gathered speed, we had to hold on to each other as it got faster and faster. This was known as going to a wedding. When anyone new to the game was on the drum it was slow and very well controlled. This was "going to a funeral." Stopping this drum, which held one thousand gallons, took some skill. On the count of three, we would all have to turn and face the other way, steady the drum then walk against it. None of us ever fell off, though we were warned many times of the danger.

This game, like our doppies, we took home with us but it never caught on with the other city school friends.

Oupa grew mainly flue-cured "Virginia" tobacco on his farm. He ran his farm very efficiently with the help of his boss-boy and seventeen other African men. Most of the European farmers grew Virginia tobacco while the African farmers grew Burley which is sun-cured. The reason being mainly, I think, the initial cost involved in the buildings.

If the rains were on time, an early shower falling in mid-November, this would boost the seedling's growth in the seed-beds, also the lands would be moistened. The young healthy tobacco plants were then planted out into the weed-free, fertilized lands. We were sometimes lucky enough to return at Easter when the picking and curing was taking place. The pink flowers and any side shoots would be nipped off. Often a few of the bigger lower leaves were picked and curing would start slightly earlier than the main crop. Oupa's bright new tractor, bought with last year's tobacco money, pulled a long trailer bringing all the men, women, and older children. On the trailer, too, were four-foot-long poles, straight and stripped clean of their bark from years of use. The tall green tobacco plants stood in straight neat lines. The Africans, armed with balls of jute baling twine, walked to the far end away from the trailer. The leaves were neatly broken off the main plant and tied in "hands" as close as an inch and a half to the end. The hands were then opened out and hung over the four foot poles. When that was covered, it was laid on the trailer. The boss-boy kept a keen look out for anyone slipping behind the others. When the set rows were completed the trailer was loaded up with the poles and the men. The women were not needed anymore and made their own way home. The loaded tractor made its way steadily back to the barns. The most surefooted man would climb to the highest point of the barn using the stronger poles which were built into the wall as a ladder. A chain of men, passing the tobacco covered poles to him, sang in their deep harmonious voices. The African on the trailer sang the main verse, which was no more than a few lines, the others brought up the chorus. A mile away the kitchen boy was smiling to himself in the kitchen as their splendid powerful voices simultaneously reached the highest beam and him.

The task done, the Africans with one exception, the boss-boy, stood stripped to their waist tired and worn out from labouring in the sun. Their black bodies shining with sweat, they picked up their shirts. The cook-boy banged the welcoming sound on the plough disc. The echoing 'dong' from the next door farm could be heard faintly between the louder dongs of our plough disk which was suspended from a tree near the kitchen door. The men walked, kicking up small clouds of white dust with their bare feet, to their compounds. Their wives awaited their return. On the open fire there would be an old round five gallon paraffin drum heating the water for a wash before they all sat down to their meal of Sadza. (Sadza—very thick stodgy porridge, perhaps to most a little bland, made from maize meal (mealie meal) and water, a friend once remarked it was like Bloody Putty!)

Willy enjoyed being with Oupa and Adam more than playing with us girls. These particular holidays were a busy time for all the men, there was some urgency about it. Willy and Adam were working amongst the Mukwa poles in the ceiling. The heat generated from the tin roof meant they were only able to work from after breakfast till half past ten, then again from half past three until dark. The timbers in the roof were not factory dressed treated timber but made out of trees cut, the poles chopped to the right length, stripped of their bark and creosoted to protect them from white ants' (termites). Ouma, thankful for their help, said nothing about the dust and rat droppings, but was more thankful when it rained because so long as the men had a steady supply of tea they worked all day. During the following few days the work went on. Behind the workshop barns was a large green "Lister" generator bolted down to railway sleepers. Gradually, we noticed large grey wires hanging down from the centre beams like grey rat's tails. The insulation was peeled back and two bare wires forked like a snake's tongue. Some of the same grey wire came out of the eaves at the back of the house and to lift it off the ground, was tied to the large high branches of the two Jacaranda trees on its way to the workshop. Then once the light fittings were fitted to the hanging rat tails, things stood still.

Willy had no more work to do on the farm, so having him with us we were able to venture further from the farmhouse. Betty, Willy, and I were good companions. Betty went to boarding school because she lived with Ouma and Oupa. While visiting the many new places Betty had found, we exchanged all our term news. It was also a good time to meet some of our old acquaintances. Ouma's pigs were growing well and getting fatter on the excess skimmed milk combined with the rough husks left after Oupa had milled his own maize meal, which he used for the Africans' rations. Even so, we always took a good supply of stale bread with us when we visited them. The pigsties were not too far from the back door and there were only three. Oupa would buy the pigs as piglets and Ouma liked to watch them grow. Very often when they were sent for slaughter we would have bets as to their weight. Ouma was always closest. Hearing us walk up the path, they would all start grunting and snorting. As they got older, they would put their front trotters on the high outer wall and greet us with their soft, square, pink noses, the milk foaming from their mouths like a white stubby Father Christmas beard.

A 'kwe-voel' (go-away-bird) distracted our attention, throwing all our bread to the pigs, we ran off to the orchard, mimicking the large grey bird. The go-away-bird was a menace. Not only did it eat a large amount of the fruit but it also devoured the flowers and tender budding spring shoots. Between feeding, it sat proudly in the tree, displaying its comb; the well drawn-out nasal explosive 'go-away' cry is quite a well-known sound. These birds were the only ones Ouma would allow Willy to shoot and even then with nothing stronger than a kattie (catapult). The garden boy was even allowed to have a kattie, armed with a few well selected stones, he went about watering the fruit trees while keeping an eye out for the pesky birds. The trees were planted in rows with neat moats dug around them; these were joined together with deep furrows. The orchard was on a very slight slope. The tap was opened and the hose pipe lay at the first tree the water would run past the nearest tree along in the furrows till the last tree.

When that tree's moat was brimming, starting from the two farthest trees from the tap the outlet of the tree in front was closed off with a shovel full of dagga (mud) and so on till the tree nearest the top was watered. A hose pipe was then placed at the next line of trees. The trees were watered once a week and it would take all day. No animals were allowed in the orchard, though the wasp-stung fallen fruit was picked up and given to the pigs.

A barbed wire fence kept the cows that were in the next field out, though from time to time they did eat some of the peaches, plums, and pears that hung over the fence. The oranges and lemons were eaten by few insects. The only things I ever remember seeing on these trees were the big hawk moth larvae. These larvae were short, fat, and green with a horn that was dark brown and looked like a rose thorn but it was not sharp, it only looked menacing. These larvae ate the leaves. Oupa often went out into the different fields with the bakkie (pickup), blowing his hooter (car horn). The cows would come from everywhere as he usually had rock salt or salt blocks for them. Some of the older cows had names, one cow or rather young bull; we named appropriately Comma. He was sleek black and on one hindquarter he had a perfect white comma. Seeing him from the orchard, we thought we would go and renew our acquaintance. He was lovely and so friendly that last time we met. Not realizing that he was, of course, several months older now, we crawled under the barbed wire and walked towards him calling him by his name. Comma stopped eating, lifted his head, and walked towards us. Pleased at the thought that our friend had not forgotten us and really proud, we quickened our step. Betty was the first to notice that Comma too had quickened his step and shouted "Stop! I don't think he looks all that friendly." We stopped dead and looked at Comma, his head went down sharply and he broke into a full canter. We all turned, almost falling over each other as we sprinted towards the fence, the bull snorting loudly behind us. By the time we had got to the fence we were in one straight line. We dived under the fence and ran for cover behind one of the fruit trees. Comma stopped short at the fence pawing the grass and breathing noisily. Only then did I realize that my skirt was still on the barbed wire fence. None of us dared to go anywhere near the fence. I did not want to face my mother either. I promised Willy I would never ever touch his Dinkies or ride his bike again, if only he would fetch my skirt. Comma did eventually walk away from the fence and I fetched my tattered skirt. My mother was very cross about my dress and Oupa said Betty should have known better than to let us go into a field with a bull in it. He was, after all, put in there to service the cows and he would have seen us as a threat to his harem.

Some days were more eventful than others. Some we spent playing in the white sand, building roads and dams under the Jacaranda trees. Willy would bring out his Dinkies, always having the best for himself or so we girls thought, we would play for ages pretending to be neighbouring farmers. The day was spent quietly. To relieve our cramped legs, we would often wander off leaving all our toys.

Separating the house from the vegetable garden was a very large cactus growth. Snakes of all types found it the best haven. We kids, though we liked the fruit, never ventured anywhere near the place not because of the snakes it harboured but because the prickly cactus had its own defences. Our servant had rather an ingenious method of robbing it of its fruit. It was a long pole with an empty tin can tied to it. One would place the fruit in the can and give a sharp twist—the pear would fall into the can. Then they were put into a basket and peeled in the kitchen sink. The prickly pear is about three or four inches long and is oval in shape. Holding it with a fork, you cut the ends off then slit along it, using a clean fork you can get the pear out. Alternatively, you roll it round in the sand like the baboons do to get rid of all the fine cactus hairs, and then peel the thick green skin off. Nearly always, this method would result in at least one hair being left in your hand.

Christmas was near now. Ouma was making the Christmas pudding and everyone had saved their "tickies" (sterling silver threepenny bits each year these became more and more difficult to find and were eventfully replaced by sterling silver charms) to put in the pudding. Christmas pudding was the only food we were ever allowed to smash and mix, this found the charms before they broke a tooth; if we ever tried to do this with any other food Adam yelled, "Your plate is not a cement mixer". It was Christmas Eve and still the light bulbs hung like lifeless blown glass balls. After supper, our evening meal, the grown-ups all sat in the sitting room listening to the radio. We had guests so all the kids were in the bedroom. We were having a pillow fight. We noticed that Oupa, Adam, and the other man were not talking. We stopped, thinking that they were coming in to quieten us, then the back door opened and closed and we continued our game.

As the faint murmur of an engine reached us there was a flash—lightning? No! Oupa had brought electricity by means of a Lister generator to our Tilly lamp, candle-lit farmhouse. (Tilly lamp is slang for paraffin lamp.) I dived under the pillow, slowly bringing my head out and seeing everyone else staring at the light. Willy was the first to shout, "We did it!" And with that we all ran into the sitting room. Ouma was putting out the Tilly lamps and my mother and the other lady were walking to the kitchen with the large brass candlesticks almost as if it was morning and nothing of importance had happened. The men came in talking and Oupa enquired if the generator was powerful enough to get lights to the barn. Willy, still excited, ran to them shouting, "We did it!" Adam said he was not to be rude; they were talking. Soon, for us too, the light switch was commonplace. Electricity in the house was Ouma's Christmas present.

Christmas Day is a very colourful day. After lunch, almost as though the day was to become just another day, the silence is broken by loud singing and dancing. The Africans, from the very oldest, a grey-haired bearded man, who claimed to know where Lobengula buried his treasure, to the youngest baby on his mother's back, would congregate at the back door. Some carried drums, others old syrup tins with a stick handle and stones rattling inside. Others, like the bearded grey man, would just hold out his jam tin, empty by now, but it had had his homemade African beer in it.

The small children would form a small circle and dance and chant. While in the larger circle, the women did most of the dancing. They could keep this up for as long as you cared to stand and be entertained. We never joined in, it was just not the done thing, but they did get our feet tapping. Standing at the top of the backdoor step, we watched them. The younger, newly married African women brought their babies up to show us. Usually the baby was wearing as many of the old baby clothes as possible, which we had given to them.

Before they left, we would throw money and handfuls of sweets into the performing group. The children dashed about wildly, picking up the hard boiled sweets and the women and men picked up all the money. The older Africans would not waste their time looking for money but came to the step to wish us a Happy Klistmass, and we in turn would thank them saying, "Please call again," and hand over an old shirt or jersey, sometimes even money. Africans find it very difficult to say their Rs so 'curry and rice' is always 'cully and lice.'

Having paid for our entertainment we walked away, saying how old this one looked or how surprised we were that the old boy was still with us and wondered if he really did know where Lobengula hid his treasure. Few of the older Africans rarely know how old they are in years, they relate their age to events of the time. Even the not-so-old farm boy, if you asked him how old his child was, he would either say he was born the year we had no rain, or perhaps say something like, "My child, she came to me when you bought your new blue car." To us these things are often irrelevant and we would have to stop and think which blue car or when did we have a severe drought which would tie into the apparent age of his child.

Maybe the reason why this farm made more of an impression on my mind is because it was the last farm at which I was to visit Ouma and Oupa; I was shut out of their lives in 1968. I received news in February 1984 that Oupa had died in South Africa. Counting back to my last year at school when he was very ill, almost dying of a brain tumour, he was about seventy-four then, this would make him aged eighty-six.

Ockert was born in September 1963 by which time we had been living in a 'Pisa' at 9 Harrow Road, Queens Park West, for nearly a year. I had returned to the school which I had been to five years ago. Newmansford School was only a short distance away from our house; Northlea was also a lot closer for Willy. A Pisa is a single storey house, many of which were built when there was a boom of immigrants into Rhodesia shortly after the Second World War. These houses were only expected to be temporary homes but some are still homes today, many years later. The early Pisa had tall elephant grass thatched roofs with no ceilings. All the walls were nine inches thick and constructed with the help of two planks. The planks were placed nine inches apart and the space between was filled with mud and straw. When the mud had hardened the planks were taken away, leaving a wall. The inside walls were made in the same way. The basic idea originated from the African Pole and Dagga huts. These were made by placing the poles very close together then plastering them over with dagga (mud). As a lot of people started to buy these once owned government houses, the banks insisted that they become more modernised before they would lend money for their purchase. Most houses were modernised forty years ago. The old wooden window frames were taken out and smart, more durable, metal ones were fitted. The corners were squared up and most houses had their thatched roofs replaced with corrugated asbestos sheets the houses became instantly cooler. The other specification was that the roofs had to have rain guttering fitted to them. The average stand was a quarter of an acre and ours was no exception. It was set to the back of the block, so we had a lovely lawn to play on. Football was the 'in' game. However we were never content to just dribble the ball along the ground, it had to be kicked high into the air. Along the grass verge between the road and our fence we had very large six feet tall sisal cacti. The large white powdery green leaves ended in needle sharp spikes on which our ball was often impaled.

The diamond mesh fence was covered all through the summer with a beautiful coral creeper. The little flowers hung like salmon pink pearls. Everyone admired our fence. This was the main reason why, when it went to seed, not ever having any pocket money, I went around selling the seeds to the other children at school. This worked very well until my mother put a stop to it.

Ouma Benadie lived in a number of government flats at this time there were some flats not too far from us. To get to her house we had to walk through a large empty plot which had a thorn tree in it. The tree was most of the time dull and almost black, like fire burnt charred limbs with large long white thorns that looked like the burnt ash at the end of the wispy sticks on a bigger log in the fire. In the spring, just before the rain in November, the thorn tree got its flowers, hanging down like delicate elongated balls of cotton wool. The flowers changed their colour as they got older, light pinks and mauve, turning yellow. The very twisted pods were dark brown, clustering at the end of a long stem. The green fern like leaves soon covered the tree and gave shade to any small shoots under its canopy.

One day, as Willy came through the gate from school so did a flea bitten dog. Willy told my mother that the dog had just followed him.

The truth came out much later: Willy had seen an African with this pathetic animal and bought the dog from him. The dog was so badly infested with ticks and so very thin that my mother felt sure he was ill. Willy was told he would have to take the dog to the police station and report it as a lost dog. Willy would not do this knowing that its owners would not be found and the dog put to sleep. Adam came home and Willy was ordered to take the dog to the police station. The dog seemed to sense his fate and broke loose as we got it to the station. One of the police dogs, which was in season at the time, was used to entice him out of a thicket. Willy went back daily till the dog was sent to the RSPCA (royal society for the protection and cruelty to animals).

His coat was beginning to shine and he looked a lot fatter. My parents didn't want him because he was an Alsatian. He would cost too much to feed properly that was the excuse they used.

At the back of our house, we had a lean-to, just poles and slats of wood with wire mesh nailed on top. In the hot summer months, the loofah creepers provided shelter from the sun. Once the bright yellow flowers died, the small green loofahs started to grow. When they were a little shorter than a continental cucumber and a little fatter, the creeper started to die. We then picked the loofahs and dried them. Peeling the hard fawn thin outer casing off, we shook out all the marrow-like seeds. They were now ready for use in the kitchen as pot scourers or in the bathroom as a 'tingle pad.'

Hedgehogs were, at one time, as common as the Tjongololos, pronounced Chongololo (millipede) that they ate. Taking it to school one day provided a very disruptive day. They are mainly nocturnal, but as we gave it a steady supply of cut worms and legless grasshoppers, he ate most of the day. Cut worms live under the ground and literally cut a plant off from its roots. They are short, fat, white segmented worms with hard reddish-brown heads.

Unfortunately, our Pisa was not looked after and the white ants started to attack the inner walls the straw provided them with an abundance of easy food. Very long and deep cracks started to appear like those one sees in the side of a cliff face. The house was condemned as it became unsafe to live in. We moved shortly before the end of 1963. Though we moved into Queen Park East, I was able to stay at Newmansford School.

The only thing that stands out about this house was the very large moon-like craters in one bedroom's outer wall. Our neighbours' servant explained them to our servant. (When I think back to how we thought we were all living within the privacy of our own homes; each of us thinking that the neighbours knew nothing of our business. One only had to ask one's servants to find out any gossip and, within minutes, one would have enough to fill many volumes and we would have our very own soap opera.)

The previous occupants had left the country in a hurry and whether it was done deliberately or by pure accident I don't know, but they had locked their dog in the bedroom. The dog, had been left, not having any food or water it tried to dig its way through the wall. We did wonder why the poor animal did not put all his efforts into one hole. Had he done so, he would have freed himself. The one hole was so close, Willy punched it with his fist in temper and it went through revealing the bright sunlight. The neighbours' attention was drawn to the house by the foul smell of the dog's rotting carcass. The police were called and the distended putrid carcass was taken away and burnt.

We only stayed in this house for a very short time. We then moved into another house, still in Queens Park East, immediately opposite Thomas Rutland School. As there was only a few weeks of term left, I still went to Newmansford.

Adam had a job at the power station but the wages were very poor. The rent was very much cheaper in this house because it belonged to the Power Station. Adam's drinking did not help. During our very short stay, my mother made clothes from extremely cheap material and sold it to the ever growing market for second-hand clothes. The police arrived one day and put a stop to her enterprise. One is allowed to sell second-clothes but she was selling new ones and that required a licence. The material was so cheap that once washed they resembled old clothes fit for floor rags; the colours had ran and the fabric was limp like a wet feather. She could not sell them to make up the money spent on the material.

Willy was still sickly but it was while we lived in this house that he was taken to hospital. He had been off school for most of 1964. Just before Christmas, I went into his room to check if he needed anything. Willy was having a fit of sorts. He ran full pelt at the wall. I ran screaming down the passage, but by the time my mother and I went back to Willy, he had knocked himself out.

Willy was taken away in an ambulance. For a long time, I was told he was not allowed to see anyone. My parents only telephoned the hospital. Willy, they thought he had rheumatic fever but later it was said that he had cerebral malaria. When he came home, he was thinner than ever and spent a long time convalescing at home. Now, when he gets a violent headache the only drug which appears to relieve the pain is medication containing quinine; this was widely used in the treatment of malaria. Willy at almost 60 still occasionally gets these very violent headaches which serve as a reminder of his youth.

A New World

The school term had started in January 1965, but Adam was contemplating another move, so we were not sent to school. Besides which Willy was still too ill. Adam applied for a position at Hippo Valley Sugar Estates. Leaving the power station and Bulawayo, we moved to a New World.

Chiredzi and Triangle were to be our homes for the next four years. Chiredzi lies some three hundred miles from Bulawayo and was referred to, by the optimists, as the Capital of the Lowveld. All our goods and chattels were transported by road and because they would take a week to arrive at Chiredzi, we visited Zimbabwe Ruins outside of Fort Victoria for two days.

Arriving at Zimbabwe Ruins in the late afternoon, we settled for a relaxed evening in the chalet. We girls and Ockert went with my mother for a bath at the main ablution block. Adam and Willy had their bath after dinner. The chalets were large and spaciously cool. They all had thatched roofs and a small wooden stove, used for cooking and heating the small hot water tank in the kitchen.

The National Parks provided an African to do one's cleaning and lighting of fires. One paid for his services on a daily basis. This left us all day to explore the ruins and surrounding areas.

Waking early the next day, we had a good breakfast, made our beds and with a packed lunch, we walked along the well made footpaths to the main ruins—The Great Enclosure. The outer wall is thirty foot tall. It towered above in a stately way encircling the main Valley Ruins.

Visitors have always maintained, as they walked through the widened gaps, that were once small tunnels, that an inner peace fell upon them. As we walked through the gap in the wall, our party fell silent. The sun was hot, very hot, the grass on the outside was wheat-coloured in parts, but within these walls, the grass was green and soft. The whole arena was cool. It was as if we had walked into some great abbey and people were kneeling. A feeling of tranquillity surged from every stone, which were placed one on top of another, without mortar of any sort. While walking through the different passages, we all spoke in whispers. My parents wondered how and why a civilization so capable had died leaving no records.

Seeing these stone buildings now, and looking at pictures of the Incas in far away South America, I can't help but wonder if Atlantis had indeed sent people to the four corners of the world. The basic idea is so much alike. Fortifying themselves in high vantage points like The Acropolis, as did The Incas who took to the hills when the Spanish invaded their land, building high stone walls, they used the hills and mountains to their advantage. Perhaps we did, at one time, all come from the same tribe. The Conical Tower intrigued me. Tugging at my mother's dress, I quietly asked, "What's inside there?" I remember, in the few seconds while waiting for her reply, I had answered myself. (I had this beautiful picture beginning to build up in my mind. It had all the mysteries of *Alice in Wonderland* and all the colour of Aladdin's cave). Far away, as if someone else was talking came this sharp interruption. "Nothing." My thoughts were back to earth with a thud. I thought to myself, that can't be right. Why was it built for nothing? Not daring to say "you lie outright," I asked, "Can I go inside?" My mother said, "Lady Jane, if you can find a way in, by all means go inside and see for yourself." Walking round and round, willing an opening, I was left standing at the tower. There was of course, no opening. The tower was once higher than its present height of thirty-three foot. The fifty-six foot base gave it stability against the elements but the builders never foresaw the greed of treasure hunters. In their obsession to enter, they had tried to climb in through the top. This is not allowed now; in fact, no one may climb on any part of the ruins. Although reading the many books written on the Zimbabwe Ruins, I still find it difficult to conceive that there is nothing inside this tower. Why, with all our modern technology, can we not see into this tower's heart without disturbing it? The Egyptians pyramids were built to house their most noble kings, so too these people may have built towers in honour of their most noble. All the records and artefacts may well be right there. Perhaps we should, as William of Ockham's philosophy suggests, "Search for the obvious and do not look to the far distance for your answers."

The next place to visit was the Acropolis. This was done in two parties. Dragging the pushchair posed too many problems. Adam, Willy, and I went first while my mother stayed down in the valley with the three little ones. Looking down one could see the magnitude of the entire ruins, not only the Great Enclosure, but many smaller ruins scattered as far as the eye could see, and in the far distance, the shimmer of a blue haze, almost as if the sky had come down and met the land too soon. Noticing the different tones of blue, we asked if that was Kyle Dam and could we go and see it. Adam said that would have to keep for another day.

When my mother and Adam returned from their trip up the Acropolis, we all sat on the short cut grass and had our picnic lunch. In the afternoon, we visited the Karanga Village. The village was made in this century. It was not only a replica of a typical Kraal (family commune—small village) but it also had museum exhibits. As has most kraals they too had a witchdoctor. For a fee you were told your fortune.

The witchdoctor sat on his haunches, bare with the exception of his very furry hat, leopard loincloth, and strings of beads and bones round his neck. Most white people did, at one time, regard these people with contempt, but they do posseses something which very few people have been able to explain; some say it is merely the power of suggestion. Unlike the fortune-teller that once told my fortune from a Turkish coffee cup, this witchdoctor's predictions were quite feasible:

    a.   I was to marry a foreigner;
    b.   Should like two children but will have three;
    c.   My family and I were to go over many waters.

My mother scorned me for wasting my money on such rubbish. It became a long-standing joke. Marry a foreigner—well, everyone was a foreigner, even I was, though I was the third generation born in the country and regarded myself to be Rhodesian just like him. Go over many waters—Adam said the only water I was likely to see was the water in my bath, then again I could jump over it many times.

The incident was soon forgotten as we moved on to the curio shop and then on to the tea room. As the day started to draw to a close, the hustle and loud chatter of the people slowly died down. The squeak of that pushchair's wheel, that needed oil, was no longer to be heard. The loud shriek of the children was suddenly missed. Then, as we sat on the park bench, the sun was beginning to set. It was time we made our way back, too, back to the chalet. While walking, Ockert had fallen asleep in his pushchair. Gretha was on Adam's back and Willy carried Petro. The loud mating call of the crickets, rasping their hind legs against their bodies, filled the air. As we settled into our chalet, the little ones in bed, the night's cool air swept through the open door, bringing with it the sound of the frogs croaking. Two people walking to the ablution blocks brought a premature lull in the chorus. Even the crickets, whom seemed to be undaunted and never ceasing, stopped. The uneasiness of silence was short lived, as soon the whole chorus started on what seemed a louder note.

It was bed time for Willy and me, we went off to bed without question because of the promise of a visit to Kyle Dam the next day. We were woken at six by cars drawing into and out of the area.

Kyle Dam was still waiting to be seen. With our picnic lunch packed in the car we drove to the Dam Wall. It was only completed in 1961 and was opened by the Honourable. Sir Edgar Whitehead, Rhodesia's Prime Minister at the time, on the 13 May 1961 the dam wall being only four years old at the time of our visit no cars were allowed on it. Parking our car in the space provided, we walked along the top. The hills in and surrounding the dam on one side were green with outbreaks of granite rocks. On the other side was a steep drop of one hundred and ninety feet into the Mtilikwe gorge. It was thought then that the water would never reach the spill gates but it did. In late 1970, the sluice-gates were opened for the first time.

Kyle was, at first, built to supply water to the surrounding parched land but it is now also a tourist attraction. The International Black Bass fishing competition is held here yearly. Unlike the English, we eat most of our coarse fish and bass is no exception. It is eaten by both Europeans and Africans alike. Having very few bones, it is easy to fillet and tastes very much like Cape Whiting.

Our family rose at five. We were the alarm clocks this day. It was the day we had to move on to our New World. We packed our car and headed back towards Fort Victoria, turning left towards Ngundu Halt. Sixty miles from Fort Victoria, we arrived at the end of the good tar road. The car's tank full of petrol, the water checked and oil alright, we almost forgot the water bags. Willy went to the little store and asked the storekeeper to fill our bags. The water bags were most important. If we should break down there's no telling how long it would be till someone came along. I am not altogether sure where the water bags originated and as I got older and more plastic containers were used the sight of water bags got fewer. They were very thick Hessian bags, but they had no special lining of plastic or waterproof material. The bags were usually twelve inches long and nine inches wide with a heavy rope handle and a very ordinary cork stopper fitted into a hole in a top corner. The only instructions that one got with a new bag was to immerse it completely in water for about twelve hours. This made the Hessian swell and very little water ever leaked out, in fact it was the slow evaporation of the water that kept the water very cool. Most cars had them hanging from the wing mirrors or the front bumpers.

The journey towards the Lowveld was very long, hot, and dusty. Once, while visiting some friends in Bulawayo, I overheard Adam telling of our first trip to Chiredzi: We were going down this dusty road and in front of me, right in the middle of the road, Man, I saw these two ears; I thought, what luck, we can have rabbit pie for dinner. When I got closer it was a great big kangaroo sitting in a pothole. A tremendous exaggeration, but the road was very bad. (Africa does not have kangaroos in the wild.)

On our arrival, we had to go to the main and original Hippo Valley Mill. The transport truck bringing our furniture had already arrived early that morning. While my parents were in the main office, we sat in the reception office having a very welcome cold drink. A laboratory technician came into talk to the lady who had given us a drink. Shortly afterwards, he asked Willy and I if we would like to see his laboratory pets.

Following him, we went into a very large room and on the top of some cupboards, running the length of the room, were two large glass tanks. Inside one was a long fat brown scorpion. We were told that he was over a foot long from his extended pincers to the tip of his sting. The other tank had his mate in—she was much smaller. Scorpions, we were told were very common in the Lowveld. We never heard of these two pets dying while we lived there and I, at times, wonder if they will become famous in a film called Scorpion, much like Bees. Our home, like so many other things, was new. Within the confines of our fence, there was a great many things to do and discover.

Arriving at our new home, which had not quite had the finishing touches put to it, we smelt the fresh paint and looked through the large, glazed, putty stained panes. The garden was uncultivated and bare with only the odd stump and larger trees that were left when the site was cleared to allow the builders access.

The larger trees I felt sure were Masasa trees. Though, now conversing with Willy, I find that Masasa trees grow mainly in the plateau areas, the trees most common to the Lowveld were Mopane. Though this is true, I can't remember being infested by Mopane flies. These flies are much smaller than the common house fly and are a real menace; they are attracted to any form of moisture and usually hover round your face, given the slightest opportunity they would be in your eye. Flying in swarms of thirty or more, these flies were named by us (Rhodesians)

Mopane flies as they seemed to be mostly around the Mopane tree. I am not sure why.

Entering the house from the side one went through the veranda. Supported by a low wall, it was gauzed in with fine wire gauze. It offered little protection against the mosquitoes, although this was its intended purpose. Once through the outer door, one could either walk into the sitting room through a double French door or the dining room through yet another such door. The sitting room was separated from the dining room by a small low internal wall, some two feet high, jutting out from either side, having a space in the middle. In many houses, the space above the wall was filled in with decorative bamboo or shell string curtains.

We never had the money for such extravagant purchases, but when Adam visited the County Club, which was often, Willy and I would collect all the crown type bottle tops. We customised our own musical string curtain, far more colourful than any bamboo. The string hung from a pole the bottle tops were bent over the cascading string hanging like coloured jewels in the smugglers cave as they were clamped tightly so they did not slip down out of place.

Well fitted for its time and referred to as an American kitchen led off the dining room. A New World gas stove stood sparkling in the kitchen. My mother looked at it with uneasy reservations, how would she get on with a gas stove? Why could she not have her old electric stove? My stepfather had explained that to her before we had arrived. The electricity supply was never intended for domestic use, so as to cut down where possible, people were asked to use gas or paraffin appliances. It was company policy to supply a gas stove. Opening the back stable door, we looked out on a maze of blinding galvanised water pipes which had not yet been buried. (PVC – [Poly Vinyl Chloride] type pipes were only used much later—1972 onwards). It was around the end of January when we arrived, still very hot and the water out of these pipes was scorching.

The stark grey cemented unpainted "Kaffir-Khaya" wall obscured the view of the empty plot. (The word Kaffir-Khaya is not used at all now. In fact it was considered almost as a swear word as was Kaffir. Perhaps I ought not to use the word but it was a word of the era and was widely accepted. It means Servant's House. The word Kaffir was found too offensive to use years prior so most referred to the house at the bottom of the garden as The Boys-Khaya but that too became unacceptable in our world of political correctness; it's the Servant's Quarters or House.)

Looking out of the bathroom window a boiler could be seen against the back wall which heated the water used in both the kitchen and bathroom. The fire was lit every day by our garden boy. Leading from the dining room was a passage. The first left was the bathroom, then between that and the next door, which was the PK (piccaninny khaya—piccaninny means small khaya means house—meaning the small house—the toilet), my room on the right, shared by my two half sisters Gretha and Petronella. (Gretha born 1961 Myrna born 1953). I was secretly afraid of the dark and having my two younger sisters in my room with me, who openly admitted to being afraid, gave me a sense of duty towards them. I can't ever remember asking for my own room.

The next door on the right was my parents' room. That, like Willy's room at the end of the passage, had a door leading out on to another gauzed-in veranda. Willy never shared his room with Ockert, because being so young at the time, he was into most cupboards. I always remember Willy owned most, if not all, the books in our house. This veranda in a neighbouring house was barricaded off and used to house the Lady of the house, when she contracted T.B. The veranda became her sanatorium for the duration of the illness. The bedroom, (which in our house was Willy's); here it was used as their quarantine and sterile area. Staff would dress and undress whilst tending her needs. To begin with, it was the talk of the township. T.B. was not unheard of in the European population; however, was certainly not the norm. As days turned into months the outside fascination waned.

We had been there a short while, when after the new sugar mill was put into operation between Chiredzi and Hippo Valley, the houses were fitted with one air conditioner free, others could be purchased at the expense of the tenants. Adam, working shift work, had to sleep during the day and so the air conditioner was fitted in his room. Often when he had been sleeping with it on, he would forget to switch it off we kids would sneak into this room and do our homework. My mother would be sure to find us out and send us on to the veranda where she said it was a lot healthier as the air was fresh and unmanufactured by a machine.

At the corners of the house, to catch the rainwater from the guttering and down pipes, were hollowed out cement slabs. It was one of my favourite pastimes to lift these up and inspect the life underneath. The ground was always cool and damp. Large flat shimmering green centipedes would snake vigorously to cover from the direct sunlight. I was always sure to lift the slab up towards me, so that my bare feet were protected by the slab. Often there would be a scorpion, they were less timid. Their tails would curl up in defence and they would dart this way and that way often going into reverse. Their pincers quivering like the lobster antenna before disappearing down their half-moon hole in the ground. Most of the scorpions that I found were the dark brown type and although their sting was painful, not fatal, like that of the black scorpion. If stung by this little scorpion, which seldom grows to more than a few inches, one would need medical help. The sting is treated like a highly venomous snake bite.

Shortly after our arrival, the trees that were still living had to be painted from the ground level to two feet up their stems, with white lime wash. Termites would build their earth road maps up the tree trunks and as they went they destroyed the soft sap wood starving the tree of its nutrients. Looking out of the bedroom window, the trees looked like one footed tennis players with their white socks. The lawn would soon be green with the coming rain next November and then it would be a good time to prepare the back garden for vegetables as before that the ground was too hard and would need a lot of effort and a good pick to crack the sun-baked earth.

Chiredzi had its own nightmares. Willy, by now was at boarding school and any signs of guilt I felt all those years ago when he got beaten in Wankie were nowhere to be found. I was trying my best to just serve. By this time, I was beginning to wonder perhaps this was what being a child was all about. Perhaps one had to be hit to within an inch of their life. After all, to learn, you need to remember the punishment otherwise why would you receive the punishment? You have to perhaps have blue black marks on your body and as they turn a sharp deep yellow tinged with green you can recall vividly how, when, and why that happened to you. Never being allowed to associate with any other children we could not compare our home life to their life. I was twelve years old and would have one more year at the local school before joining my brother at Fort Victoria High School. My school, unlike my brother's large sophisticated one, was to be a Church garage. Ten, eleven, and twelve-year-olds were all to be taught in the one room by the same teacher.

Our lessons were, of course, very general and much of the time was spent outside under the trees—the garage being very poorly ventilated and the temperatures rising to 120 ºF. It was very pleasant outside and one could hardly be blamed for not concentrating on the little more than difficult lessons. After all, if you did, you would never notice the little dung beetle making her way backwards through life, collecting the cattle dung increasing, slowly, her perfect ball. The dung beetle laid its only egg in the dung for two reasons—to ensure a plentiful supply of food for its larvae, and the other as the dung decomposes, the heat given off helps its egg to hatch. The chameleon, noticing a large fly basking lazily in the shade of a leaf, moved slowly, cautiously, hesitating a while, anticipating. "Has the fly seen me, shall I put this foot down, will my elasticised tongue reach him?" Then, as if to make sure that no other competitor has seen his dinner, he rolls his cement mixer like eyes round quickly, three hundred and sixty degrees. Then without hesitation, flashes his tongue out—a sure hit. The only evidence of what had once been a fly was the slight stirring of the leaves.

The Africans loathe the chameleon, but in spite of this, they would never actually kill one. They believe that when God created the world he made all the people dark skinned, like them. Then God made the animals. God then sent the different animals to different groups of people. The fastest animal, the cheetah, was sent to the European races, and so on down the line. When at last God came to send them their animal, the only one left was the chameleon. They say that each animal was given the same message. This message was where to find a pool of magical water in which they should bathe, naked, and when one came out of this pool one was washed white. The chameleon was sent to the group now known as the Africans; they considered themselves to be the unfortunate ones. Therefore, they arrived at the pool long after every other race. The pool had started to dry up. This is why the palms of their hands and the soles of their feet are lighter than the rest of their bodies. There was only just enough water left for them to dip these two parts in. Hence their name for the chameleon, Hamba Gashle which means 'Go slowly.' Hamba Gashle is a dialect derived from Ndebele, Shona, Afrikaans, and English, a language loosely called Kitchen Kaffir or Tsjalapalapa.

"Collect all your books and finish off the exercise at home." That was the teacher. Again I found I had more homework than anyone else in my class thanks to the distractions. Well, at least it was Friday. The plan was, homework first, then a walk and perhaps a swim in the canal.

On the way home, the clouds hung heavy in the sky. 'I had better run, for sure I'll be caught in the storm.' Nearly home and the heavens opened, up came the wind. The sky darkened by the low clouds, almost so low that they seemed to touch the larger Baobab trees, suddenly lit up with a frightening flash of lightning. It looked as if someone had turned on a light. An almighty crack of thunder followed almost immediately. 'Thank goodness, I can just see our house.' I walked in like a drowned rat, shivering mainly from fear but also cold. The power was off. I knew the lightning had hit something. As kids we would count from the time we saw the lightning to when we heard the thunder and would remark on the distance the storm was away from us; with the immediate clap of thunder the storm was on top of us. The main power line had been hit. This was nothing new and did not really affect us as we had a gas stove.

The most important part of the storm was when it was over. Like jackals, we would wait for the lion to have its fill. The storm died. Three hours after the first large splash, one and three quarter inches of rain had fallen, not quite a record. From the smallest to the largest we would emerge to gloat over someone's roof that lay in a crumpled mess on the garden or some yards away. In the four years that we lived in the Lowveld, we only heard of three roofs being blown off by just such a storm. I never quite knew whether it was the storms that mellowed or that the builders got wise to them.

A swim was out, the canals were too dirty. The storm had stirred the silt that lay at the bottom. Walking along the canal, I stopped and looked across the sugar plantation. There in the middle was left, after clearing the other trees and shrubs, what looked like a tree that had been uprooted and stuck back in the ground. It was the very thick but hollow trunk of a Baobab tree, its thick set branches and wispy twigs. It's no wonder the Africans call it the upside-down tree. The trunk looked almost lifelike, grey with hanging solid folds like a rhino's skin. After the large white rotting meat-scented flower are fertilised by the bluebottle flies in October and November, we waited for the large fruits. Cracking the very hard greenish velvet shell the many kidney shaped brown seeds scattered. The seeds had a whitish powdery substance on them and after sucking them for quite a while one was left with the kidney shaped seed. Commercially, the white powder is sold as cream of tartar. We would relish these fruits and eat dozens of the seeds. Why, I am not sure. I am certainly not able to eat commercialised cream of tartar by the spoonful.

On Thursdays, we would play sport. The church grounds having no such facilities we would, by kind permission of one of the estate managers, play hockey and football on a cleared but not quite prepared field. To this day, it still amazes me how we ever found the ball in such dusty conditions. It was one Thursday after returning from a hockey match that I found my mother both frightened and still in a slight state of shock. Gretha had been bitten by our pet monkey. I went into the room where she lay, hot and feverish, with her leg badly swollen. My mother had never taken too kindly to the idea of us having Coke, so named because he could drink a Coke faster than any of us! This fact we were always proud to show off. In her rage, my mother had given the monkey to the first passing African who quite assuredly enjoyed Coke's sometimes silly and clever antics. Gretha had just walked away from Coke and stood talking to our house boy's child, when Coke for whatever reason, attacked her, catching her, mouth bent sideways, deep on her calf muscle. My stepfather at work and not having a phone, I went through the empty plot at the back of our house and fetched the local and only chemist. Seeing Gretha and upon hearing the tale, he assumed the worst. The animal had contracted rabies—not a moment to lose. Gretha was taken to the Mission Hospital and the animal had to be found. At 3:30 a.m., Coke was found and after a rather heated argument and five dollars, the African parted with him. Coke was taken to the hospital where a white sheet and operating table were waiting for him. Coke was sadly put to sleep and his brain sent to Salisbury to be analysed. Gretha had already been given one of the twelve abdominal injections for the prevention of rabies. To our relief and Gretha's, the results were "telephoned" through on Saturday—negative.

Sometime later, we got to know Ossie Bristow who had an animal sanctuary just outside Fort Victoria near Zimbabwe Ruins. Having had the incident relayed to him he said that all primates get exceptionally vicious during the mating season and would in fact attack anyone or thing without provocation. Willy was exceptionally angry and accused us all of killing his pet. Feeling as though it was my fault entirely, I had been the one to insist Gretha had to be taken to the hospital while others were happy to wait to see how things developed. I knew rabies had to be treated within twelve hours of any contact for the treatment to be effective. I stayed clear of him for some time. Willy had a very special way with all animals. He was never afraid of any of them and could tame even the most vicious dog. If ever we arrived at a house where there was an untethered dog Adam would make Willy get out the car and greet the animal who would instinctively wag his tail and become instant friends with him.

During the school holidays when Willy was home from boarding school we, as a whole family, went out on day trips. Adam felt a certain security with Willy in toe; One of our many favourite places was Hippo pools as we named it was both beautiful and tranquil.

Leaving Chiredzi and travelling further south into the deeper, denser bush, the roads were mostly nine foot tarmac until we turned off and took the dirt road. The track, rather than a road, twisted first this way then that, only to miss the larger tree stumps that had been left when the Africans had cut the trees down for firewood. That part of the trip was slow and very dusty. Willy walked ahead of the car picking out the best routes. It reminded me of when cars were first made and they could not go faster than a man's walking pace. Some way ahead one could smell the water; now and then hear the cry of the fish eagle as it merged with the smells. The river had cut a deep gorge into the surrounding barren sun-baked land. Finding a soft sandy bed it rested a while, making a pool. Hippos taking a liking to the spot, deepened it and took it over as a playing pool.

Parking the car on the higher bank under the little shade of the few thorn trees, we walked down to the river. Down the steep sides we walked sideways like crabs each clinging on to his basket or blanket. After a short while, we felt the very soft white river sand underfoot. The hippos, snorting and grunting like contented pigs, regarded us with contempt. First one rose, blowing steaming fountains of white spraying water, then another. At first we wondered if our staying would annoy them, but then just as soon as the water surface was broken by these gigantic four-ton sea cows it settled. (In Afrikaans they are called seekoei. See—pronounced sea and means sea/ocean; koei—pronounced something like coo in cooee and means cow. The letter *C* is not widely used in Afrikaans so a *K* can have a soft or hard sound). Slight whirlpools were still evident under the water but none of them showed themselves until much later. A very large but old dead tree stood in the middle of our sandy beach. The tree bent towards the ground as if to take root once more, then straightened up again. It had no wispy twigs, just tough weathered black, grey solid branches. In its curve, we impatiently took our turn to sit, pretending as we did, to sleep and bouncing gently up and down on the natural elasticity of the tree.

The sun high, we had lunch and just enjoyed the relaxed atmosphere of the river. Higher up on the rocks the African women brought their children and week's washing. Picking out a floating raft of soap lather and giving it some grand ship's name, we willed it in and out of the rocks, racing it one against another, until its destined death, the small rapid just before the hippo's pool.

The shadows were getting longer and longer, the water taking a darker shade to it. The hippo's inner built clock stirring them, they popped up and down like floating corks grunting and snorting all the while. They were getting more and more restless submerging with deep sighs of impatience. Collecting our belongings, we decided to leave. We made our way back up the steep banks sometimes on all fours like a retreating troop of baboons. Once the things were in the car we stood at the edge and realised why the hippos were restless. The biggest bull emerged first. Once he had hollowed his bed out and was comfortable, some of the females joined him with their calves. Although hippos live mainly in the water, they do feed mainly at night. They keep the river banks reasonably clean by cropping the weeds and grass in the shallows. Hippos we were always told were generally not aggressive, in fact, quite shy. However, many years later, I watched a documentary and in there they were portrayed as being very unpredictable and extremely aggressive. I did wonder if this was due to something which man had done to these animals that appeared to us all those years ago as gentle giants or were they always aggressive. We had inadvertently encroached on their grazing ground. We spent many happy days up and down that same river, but we were always sure to leave long before sunset.

Although Adam was always one for visiting different places, once we got there, we did little else, except for one occasion. We got to hear of a beautiful spot on the Mtilikwe River. We drove for what seemed hours. We never found that particular spot but did in our minds find one which was equally beautiful.

Parking the car we went to survey the picnic site. A thin disused path, overgrown in most places, headed towards the river. Clearing the wild vines and tall elephant grass either side as we walked, with the large sturdy branches that we had picked up, we made our way slowly to the river. The path ran parallel to the river for some ten feet, making a detour to the water's edge. The small lay-bys only had room for the two men to stand side by side. It was at one of those lay-byes that we noticed a cave made from the overhanging and entwining vines. Chopping the entrance larger, we found it the perfect spot, so cool and peaceful. The leaves and vines filtered the sun while we sat inside our cave.

Adam, Willy, and a friend started the task of catching our midday meal. All went well. Lunch time was nearing and the keep-net had a few one pound and one and a half pound bass. Then it happened: "Damn it, I have caught a snake!" said my stepfather. "It's not a snake! Back up, back up, and don't let it curl round the line. You will never get it off!" his friend shouted. Adam only too eager to obey an order, backed up the path, slipped, found his footing again, and went further up the path. Carefully, one step behind the other he went up the path all the while reeling in his line and trying to keep it taut as he could. By this time, we were all at the opening of our vine/man-made cave. Closer and closer, Adam stepped towards a very innocent looking bush. He did not foresee the dangers till it was too late. Adam was caught! The wag-n-bietjie bos caught his legs! Swinging round in absolute agony, still holding firmly on to his rod with the eel still intact, he collapsed into the bush. The eel, feeling sure that he had been let off, tried desperately to slither to the safety of the water. It just became more and more tangled in the fishing line. Adam, however hard he tried to rid himself of the slimy, cold wet eel, was helpless. The wag-n-bietjie bos the literal translation means 'wait-a-bit bush' and that is really what you have to do, wait patiently while someone else unhooks its needle sharp, inward curved, hooklike thorns out of either your skin or your clothes.

The line had to be cut several times so as to free the eel, which was thrown back into the river. Adam retired into the cool of our cave and was waited upon for the rest of the day.

As the days went into months, Chiredzi was changing. Newer and larger shops were being built. The post office was to take a new shape as well. It had been a small tin rondavel (round tin or wooden hut with one door and maybe a window) with little wooden pigeon holes that housed the mail, where a solitary African sat, perspiring with the ever increasing heat drawn in by the galvanised tin roof. Within this primitive hut was also our telephone exchange. It was a small box, twelve inches square, with a head set and quite a few switches, a handle on the side which cranked it into life like a Model T Ford. It's little wonder that around midday it was almost impossible to raise the operator as invariably he was settled under a tree accepting the cooler breeze, flicking the odd fly off his face. On my way home from school, I would call in at the post office and collect the mail, if any, and pass over whatever sandwiches I had left. David always accepted these with grateful thanks, and I was allowed to collect my own mail.

The new post office was a red brick building with large grey air conditioners protruding out of its walls. A number of green boxes with numbers in gold painted on them faced the road. Sometimes I would catch a glimpse of David in his all important khaki uniform sitting at the desk sorting out the ever increasing mail that the more junior members of his team had difficulty in doing.

The most important change of all, as far as the kids thought anyway, was our new school. It consisted of three classrooms, a breezeway and two small offices. At the time we did think that it could have been built nearer, not appreciating that one day it would indeed be surrounded by houses. In our eagerness that our school should be the best in the Lowveld, we returned day after day to help plant the lawn. The African staff did the heavy digging and terracing while we planted the lush green runners of grass.

Bulldozers were brought in to clear the playing fields and then local prisoners who had been sentenced to hard labour were brought in to help plant grass on the ever increasing playing fields. (Prisoners working in the school grounds and parks were a common sight in Rhodesia.) It was on one of these afternoons that Dairy Boards refrigerators broke down and they were not able to sell the ice creams that had been spoilt. A large truck appeared and we were all given three or four half-frozen, half-melted ice creams. We all ate greedily, the bandits in the larger playing fields in their unbleached, arrow printed, calico uniforms, and us in our very colourful range of shorts and hats on the other field, labourers all, enjoying the ill fate of Dairy Board.

In order to raise funds for our ever growing little school, we made use of what was available. We had a sponsored cotton pick. Leaving Chiredzi early on Saturday morning we made our way to the Lower and Middle Sabi Development Scheme. We spent the night in a number of different houses and after a very large breakfast, with a packed lunch in our hands, we made our way to the cotton fields on an open trailer pulled by a tractor. At the appointed field, we were each given a Hessian sack and the contest started. The sponsors were firmly in our minds, we were out to make them pay. Most had promised to pay one cent per pound. We picked the fluffy white cotton out of its split pod. Most farmers still use hand pickers and these people are paid by the weight of the cotton. At the end of the day, it is recorded on their card and totalled up at the end of the week. By hand picking one is able to keep the cotton a lot cleaner. With mechanical picking you get all the dead dry leaves sticking to the cotton.

The day was long and hot; so hot that it is the only time I ever remember wearing a hat. I loathe a hat with a passion and whether it is this loathing or not I am not sure but will have the most explosions of headaches after wearing a hat for a few hours. Although we seemed to pick so many fluffy white balls our sacks never seemed to get any heavier. Some of us, and I was one of them, wished we were back in Chiredzi swimming in the canals.

We broke for lunch and sat under the trailer, shading ourselves from the sun. After lunch we were informed, to our delight, that the next field was only 20 percent ready and could leave it till a later date, which never came, to the relief of all. The rest of the day till 4 o'clock was spent in rather green slimy, but equally pleasant reservoirs, not quite as good as a swim in the canal but at least we had a chance to cool off.

The outstanding money was collected and a gift token given to one of the boys for picking the most cotton. The incident was soon forgotten as other more successful fund raising events were being thought of.

Our house stood off the main road through Chiredzi and so was one of the first roads to be tarred with real black tar and stones. Gone forever were the days when you would smell the surplus molasses waste on the roads, never again would the dust be settled by the black sticky syrup. Our road may well have fallen prey to tar but the road leading out of Chiredzi to far off places like Rutenga and Nuanetsi was still a clean dirt road, even untouched by molasses.

In the outlying districts were the big cattle ranches. Adam had a cousin who managed three large cattle ranches in the Nuanetsi area. Often we would go there for the weekend, and while there, the idea was we were able to shoot wild game. Although Adam would often swell with childlike pride as he would ask what had this one or that one thought of him as he dished out merciless punishment; did the third party think him a hard case. His tone was one of overall disappointment if one never thought of him as a hard man but the truth was he had no more killer in him then the next person he was the Bully. Our visit would coincide with Flip Meiring restocking of his wife's deepfreeze. Over the weekend he would kill, from his own stock, a pig, goat, and maybe even a cow. Once the African had skinned the animal, with skill second to none, my brother, Adam, and Flip would cut the carcass up in the cool of the evening. Fewer flies were about and also the carcass was then at room temperature. We had got most of it bagged and labelled when the silence was broken by a loud crashing at the door. The herdsman stood frightened, not only because of what he had just witnessed, but also because of his boss's reactions. "Baas, please, Baas, I am hearing too much noise from the little cows and when I get there I see that she has already killed a little one cow," he said in his broken English.

Flip, furious at the thought of losing a calf to 'she,' said in a very menacing voice, "Who is 'she,' talk to me in your own language!"

The African, being completely at ease in his own language, told Flip that a leopard had broken into the barbed wire compound and taken a calf. It was not unknown for this to happen though very few leopards would come so close to the house to collect a meal. Over the next week, a lone calf was tethered in the stockade and the biggest snare was set. The snare was made up of two half circles of flattened metal with large sharklike teeth. These were joined together by a bar of metal. It had the strength and power of a giant clam, as we were to find out later. Night after night an African sat high in a thorn tree watching and waiting for the leopard's return. The African, tired and cold and nothing appeared to be happening, fell asleep. Some say that the leopard knew he was waiting for him. Silently, the leopard stalked his prey, the young calf having been tied there for a week and having no knowledge of his purpose, stood patiently digesting his evening meal. All too late the calf sensed the uneasiness in the air, the leopard darted through the open gate, which consisted of two large thorn tree branches with strands of barbed wire strung between them. It stopped as suddenly in his tracks as he had started——the leopard had not seen the dark vile devil in its path. Click! Simultaneously the sound of crushing bones as the jaws of the clam closed, waking the sleeping African. The leopard snarled and growled in anger, tugging with the power of his other three powerful legs, he tried in vain to release his trapped paw. The African, seizing the opportunity, climbed out of his tree and ran to the house, no more than five or six hundred yards away. Flip, anticipating the reason for the horrendous banging at the back door, picked up his loaded .303 and spare shells and answered the door. Flip and the African returned in the pick-up truck. We followed in hot pursuit in the car. To our horror and total amazement, the leopard, so obsessed with freeing itself, had almost eaten its paw completely off. The leopard turned and looked at Flip with raging pain in his eyes and then turned his head. Blinking his eyes, he looked back at Flip. The pain was gone from his eyes, as if he knew that soon he would suffer no more, he looked sad and pleadingly at Flip. Flip aimed carefully and squeezed the trigger. The rifle, powerful enough to stop an elephant, echoed through the still night. The dying echo was soon replaced by incessant babbling of the Africans emerging from the nearby huts.

The African who had fetched Flip stood bravely over the dead leopard showing the beast off with pride. Then, picking up the half eaten paw, showed the large audience. The men stood, some with just trousers on and others trying to do inside-out shirt buttons up.

The women those who were rich enough to afford them, had very colourful blankets, others just in gaudy printed, un-edged squares of material wrapped round themselves, covering all but their heads. (The children, some of whom were naked were all hiding behind their mothers.) The clouds moved across the sky to reveal a splendid moon, giving the speaker just enough light. The paw in hand he told the tale of the leopard. Adding to the speaker's vivid description, the men in the audience, in their loud, deep voices exclaimed the usual "Ah, Ah, Ah, MI WIE." The women, those who weren't supporting a child on a hip, almost at right angles to their bodies like a cliff edge, cupped their hands over their mouths and murmured in low tones, "Geesaas" (Jesus). Most of the younger children stood wide eyed and bewildered, not quite grasping why their sleep had been disturbed and indeed would not have been, had their parents not caused such a commotion while trying to find suitable clothes to view the leopard, in the dead of night.

While the drama of the leopard was being enacted, the dogs, like the people, had their part to play. They provided the musical chorus. Yapping and barking, they ran round the crowd, trying to find a gap between the maze of legs. One dog broke through, his senses sharpened by the hollow in his stomach. He went single-mindedly, straight to the leopard. The African, realizing the attention of the crowd was being diverted by something else, looked at the ground, and with a violent kick sent the dog yelping, tail between its legs, back into the crowd where it had to run through a gauntlet of kicking legs and furious shouts of "foot sack" (go away). The dog sat in the shadows, dejected. Then one at a time, the other dogs ventured towards him but only drawn by the smell of blood from the leopard that spotted the sides of his mouth. The dog snarled and bared his teeth. The other dogs, warned, retreated. The Africans keep a dog only for hunting. They always appear half starved it is thought, so that they may outrun any rabbit or wild hare. So that they don't hunt for themselves at night they are tied up outside the hut. The more cunning dog, driven by sheer hunger, will chew through his rag-rope and hunt for himself, very often catching a meal. Tearing the meat from the bone in huge chunks, he would gulp it down. The dog would then, obediently, return to his post, sleep and digest his meal, tummy bulging. Then, like a python after a large meal, he would lay sleeping for the whole of the next day.

Flip, not wanting the smell of blood to attract any other animals, like hyena and jackal, as it had the dogs, told the African to put the carcass in to the back of the truck. It would have to be skinned that night; otherwise the fur would fall out in handfuls. As he drove off, the crowd slowly made their way back to the dark huts. The children were the first to settle down on their grass mats, placed neatly on the floor. Flip and the African, once back at the house, worked quietly removing the skin like skilled surgeons. Only when the carcass hung unrecognizable from the large hook in the rafters did they both pause. Flip lit up his pipe and the African fetched the coarse salt. The skin was put down, fur first, and handfuls of rock salt was thrown on to the white, wet, fleshy side. The skin was now left to dry, the salt would keep the maggot flies off it. Curing and drying the skin could take two weeks or more. Flip, to the delight of the African, gave the carcase to him and said he was to collect it in the morning, or rather later that morning.

All the sugar cane fields were serviced by a maze of canals. Once every two years the Main Canal, nine foot wide and twelve foot deep, was drained and cleaned. Gangs of African workers armed with large stiff yard brooms scrubbed the concave concrete walls of the canal. As sections of the canal was sealed off and drained a large audience gathered. Rusty, unrecognisable old bicycles were retrieved and once even a drowned zebra was found. Adam had told us, some months past, that a man, returning from the country club had missed the turning in the road and drunkenly driven his scooter into the canal. Whilst standing on the embankment watching the water level subsiding someone shouted out, "There's Joe Soaps scooter," forgetting for the moment who the man was.

Although there was the actual danger of falling in the canal, the biggest fear, though not in any child's mind, was Bilharzia. Very few people were passed over where Bilharzia was concerned. Some were left scarred for life. In my last years at Fort Victoria High, Marie, a friend from Chiredzi School, was very ill and in fact had both ovaries removed. They were so badly infested and damaged by the Bilharzia parasites. Marie is now, I am told, married and living in South Africa where I have also been told have adopted their children.

Bilharzia is carried by a small snail which lives on the inside walls of the canal. This snail carries a microscopic flatworm parasite which burrows through the pores in human skin. It travels in the bloodstream and will make its host the liver, kidneys, bladder, or bowel. Bilharzia parasites, if they are left unattended, will eventually kill their hosts. In the 1970s, a new strain, to Rhodesia, of Bilharzia was analysed from some men in the army, it lived in the brain cells. Though animals do get Bilharzia, it is not as common as in humans, their fur protects them.

Appreciating these two very serious dangers, it was decided that a swimming pool should be built. The swimming pool was not very far from our house and when Adam was on afternoon shift we were allowed to go swimming. The sweet, crystal blue water always looked very inviting and the hot afternoons provided a perfect setting, yet still we enjoyed swimming in the smaller canals.

The lowveld was expanding fast. With more people arriving, faster and more efficient transport was needed. It was decided the lowveld should have an airport. The Buffalo Range Airport was to serve, initially, Chiredzi and Triangle.

On one of our school trips, we visited the new airport. The runway was almost completed. Only being a few children, we were able to get very close to operations. During our visit, we were able to have a ride on the very large, black, steaming tar machine. The nine foot square monster moved at snail's pace, forcing melted hot tar on to the newly laid 'quarter to dust' white granite stone chips. The tar sprayed out of a length of pipe attached to the rear, which had holes at regular intervals. The entire visit became so meaningfully important when one romanticising youngster said, "Just think we are the first people ever to walk, well, not quite walk, on this runway." Later, on the 8 December 1965, the airport was officially opened by the Hon. George Wilburn Rudland, the Minister of Transport and Power. In his speech, he said something like: "I, being the first person to walk on the runway, declare it open!" Mr. Rudland looked important as he stood on the bottle green jute carpet but his speech had lost its importance and flavour. As children, we protested silently amongst ourselves. "We were the first!" While consoling ourselves with our own thoughts, which one of us put into words. "Our speech was said spontaneously, and with grandeur, while travelling on our Black, Sweet Smelling Tar Machine." The airport was soon able to handle seven hundred and thirty-seven planes but only during daylight hours.

Going to school in a small developing place like the Lowveld, the children were introduced to a great number of innovative projects and had an education which no text book could ever match. We visited a government project where Burly Tobacco was being produced. We learned firsthand how a cooperative worked. I was amazed to see how much of an important part the women played in this venture. A society where women were regarded as possessions and not for any other skills other than those required to bear and raise children. We visited on another field trip an area which was being prepared for cattle ranching. The area was heavily wooded with small stunted trees; the grass was scarce and the soil very poor having its life sapped out of it by the many trees trying to grow. Here we learned about Ring Barking. Selected trees were left for permanent shade and they were not always the biggest but they were the ones on the day that appeared the healthiest; the others had a section about three foot from the base of the tree stripped of their bark; it was explained to us that the capillaries that helped feed the very tips of every part of the tree were just below the bark leading into the sapwood. Every tree has a natural defence and healing process which would take place healing any wound but it could not recover from the nine inches of bark being stripped from it. The tree would over time die and in so doing it would not take any more water or nutrients from the soil thus leaving the stronger trees to grow more prolifically; the grass would benefit two fold. One, it no longer was competing with so many trees for food, and two, the dying trees would provide the much-needed shelter from the scotching African sun. Ultimately, the objective was achieved grazing land for the cattle ranchers. The dead trees still had a purpose they would provide the people with firewood.

The 25th of December seemed so close at hand, and once again, we would spend Christmas on the farm. Yet when I thought of joining Willy at Fort Victoria High School, January felt like a lifetime away. How I wished I was able to, magically, put the visit to the farm behind us. My mother was working well into the night to try and get my suitcase ready. I have never had so many new clothes all at once. How very important they made me feel. My mother felt I needed a new 'hair do' to offset my new clothes and because she said my hair always hung like rat's tails. I wore my hair mostly tied up as it was pin straight and very fine. Curse the person who invented the "Toni Home Perm" and double curse Shirley Temple for she was whom I had to look like to satisfy my mother. How awful I looked, a fat, round faced, pug nosed twelve-year-old with dreadfully tight curly hair that sat round my head like a balding monk's ring of hair.

Willy, being no different to any other brother, was horrid and cruel. He walked round me while I sat on that chair of torture; on the table the metal dinky curlers sat. A thin cynical smile developed on his face, and then he had a hurtful laugh in his eyes as he said, "You look, just like that nanny next door." Gladys, the next door's nanny, responding to European influence had tried, unsuccessfully, to beautify herself, adopting the European women's cosmetics and vanity. Not appreciating that within her own culture she was capable of exceptional beauty, Gladys had bought a very large Busby type wig. On Sundays, she would titivate herself and emerge hours later only to be ridiculed by the more conventional African women. I too, would be the focal point of ridicule, impersonating a dead and forgotten fashion. That perming experience was to last well into my adult years. I never tried to perm my hair again until after my second son was born 1975.

My eyes began to blur and I ran, angry and hot tempered, out of the room. As I thrust my head under the cold water tap, I had one thought in my mind. I would wash my hair until it all fell out, that sight could not be worse than all those horrible curls. The water sprayed forcefully over my head and I sobbed. How I hated everyone. My curls and I went to boarding school. At school, I found a perfect solution: while discussing what we would excel in once we all left school, a budding hairdresser was put into practice. Sometime later I emerged with a slightly shorter hair cut than Mia Farrow.

Boarding school was a sanctuary for me, like a concealed cave high in the mountains. Here I had so many different 'Times.' Adam never allowed us to play sport. He said we were at school to get an education not to learn how to play. Our sport consisted of two physical sports and one extramural activity; I joined the archaeology class and spent a lot of time out in the bush. One such field trip, we went up onto a granite hill where I came across what we called the resurrection plant. To most, it looked dead brittle and lifeless, but the instant one poured water on it, it blossomed into a vibrant green living plant. Our teacher must have been caught out before as he had a supply of fresh water at the jeep. Most of us became obsessed with finding another dead plant and resurrecting it. There was a time to play sport, time to work and most of all a time to enjoy myself. While at boarding school I entered one of my abstract paintings in the Fort Victoria Agricultural Show. While helping to set up the art exhibition, I noticed some were entering flower arrangements and asked if I could put a floral arrangement on as well; I received a special mention for both my exhibits. The different times fitted so very well together and were enjoyable. Unlike so many of the first year children, I was never sad when it was time to collect the bus that The Hippo Valley Citrus Estate provided to taxi the children to and from school. At the beginning of our second term, Adam and my mother wanted to do some shopping in Fort Victoria. The trip coincided with our return to school. Our nanny at the time also required a lift; she wanted to visit her mother at Ngomahura.

Ngomahura is a small village between Ngundu Halt and Fort Victoria. At Ngomahura is a hospital, our nanny thought it was a Missionary Hospital, but in fact, it is a government institution. From 1926 until 1966 the hospital was run by Dr. Mostert and treated many leprosy patients. Since 1966 when it was closed down as a Leprosy Hospital it was used for mental and TB patients. We left Mary at the main road to find her own way to the Leprosy Hospital; my parents said they were running short of time—that was a lie! I fear now, that their lie was an excuse for something more serious. Like many of the community, they had the same deep-seated fears and superstitions. Flu is transmitted by germs in the air. Leprosy is also caused by a particular germ. This germ is a micro-organism of the soil, living on decaying organic matter. Something scientists are still searching for is the answer, what transformed it into a very harmful germ? Though scientists have been working with leprosy for the past thirty years, they cannot answer all their own questions. Leprosy appears to have so many facets. As do people respond to the same given situation in different ways, the body reacts very differently to the leprosy germ. With some people it progresses very quickly and deforms and cripples its victims, while others are more fortunate and only have lightening patches of the skin. Before the vaccine for polio was found, it was said to be the worst crippling disease but now leprosy has taken the rostrum. With the help of many dedicated people this may not be the case in years to come. Many victims are now coming forward voluntarily, before leprosy has taken a firm hold of them. Many such people have, for generations, been told that it's because of their sins that they have leprosy. For some, it must be very difficult to denounce their own teachings and superstitions. As a child, going to Sunday school, I read in the Bible that different people had leprosy. This intrigued me, thinking leprosy to be a Biblical disease, why did we not have a cure for it? Other than the use of a similar word there is no evidence that Biblical leprosy is the disease which we call leprosy today. In fact it may very well be a misinterpretation of the ancient Hebrew word 'tsara'ath' because when Alexandrian scholars translated the Old Testament into Greek, approximately three centuries before Christ, they chose to use the word *lepra*. It is used to describe a number of things. The same misunderstanding could arise today in our modern society. We have come to recognise Athlete's Foot as a type of fungus. Hypothetically speaking, Jack not knowing what Athlete's Foot was called but knew it to be a fungus tells a friend, Joe, about a fungus growing between someone else's toes, Joe, in turn, knowing mushrooms to be a type of fungus tells a third person, "My friend Jack knows someone who has mushrooms growing on their feet." That sounds so funny and ridiculous it could almost become material for a childish joke. Shamefully, due to our thoughts of this mildly contagious disease and partly to our misconception, our choice of the word *leprosy* to explain this disease was also a short sighted and poor one. People all over the world are shunned by others because they have or have had leprosy. Leprosy, unlike cancer is not a painful disease but the suffering which derives from it goes far beyond the patient, extending into the depths of their families, still we don't feel the same compassion and sympathy as we display towards cancer, which can be a self inflicted disease the example here might be lung cancer contracted by heavy smokers. Most of the time, one can recall the reasons why a servant left or perhaps was fired. Mary was once working for my parents and then she was no longer there. Looking back on it now, it may well have been because her mother was a leprosy patient at Ngomahura.

In Zimbabwe, there were ten thousand registered leprosy patients. Only nine were Europeans and some two and a half thousand are now on the newer multi-drug programme. I would like to think Zimbabwe, like India and other countries in the world, would put their best foot forward in the fight against leprosy. The word *leper* is a word of the past, and in 1966, it was banned from "The Leprosy Mission's" title. It would be a perfect world when "The Leprosy Mission" is a thing of the past too. That can only happen when scientists find their 'wonder drug.'

On our return to school, at the beginning of the third term, our bus met the Triangle Sugar Estate school bus. There was always strong competition between our two buses as to who got to school first. The Tokwe River was flooded. The low level bridge was two foot under water. Though the bus may well have been able to pass, the fear was perhaps that, the force of the water had taken part of the bridge away.

Our African driver, enthusiastically joining in our competition, said he knew of a route which bypassed the Tokwe River. He was egged on by hoards of overexcited children, who never for one moment stopped to think. Most flash floods disappeared almost as soon as they had started, and providing the bridge was not damaged, we would have been able to pass. We did, in fact, turn round and a few miles down the road we turned left off the partly tarred road. The journey was very hot and dry. The area looked almost like a desert.

The goats roamed freely grazing on the smallest blade of dry grass and stripping any new tender shoots on the smaller trees. Small African shops dotted the dusty roadside some had plaited straw roofs covering their verandas, while the others had nothing. The black cemented floor was a sitting place for dogs, children and the local tailor and his large black Singer Treadle Machine. Around him, on homemade wire coat hangers, hung his past efforts, swaying in the gentle breeze as though they danced to an inaudible waltz, most brightly coloured dresses of all sizes.

On the side of the road, in a button-less shirt, was a piccaninny (small child) with his large pot belly protruding over his khaki shorts, manoeuvring his scaled down model of the latest American flashy car. While the female piccaninny learned, from a very early age, how to wash the clothes at the river, the males were being taught how to make very detailed wire cars. Some cars had the sophistication of solid wheels made from small 'Bata' polish tin lids, others were made from a thicker gauge wire. The master builders of these cars had built into their cars a suspension which our bus appeared to have lost when it turned off the tar road. Their cars bounced over the larger boulders then gracefully, almost in slow motion glided back to their horizontal plane. The piccaninnies imitated the whine of our engine, pride beaming over their faces, while they tried to race our noisy bus out of the village. Their small bare feet kicked up clouds of white dust as their little cars with extended steering wheels were pushed silently along the dirt track. Our bus jolted along the road, looking out of the back window, the piccaninnies stood in a single file across the road, each one pawing the sandy road with one foot sending up short bursts of dust. Then the race was on, leaving the starting line, they raced towards the finish, a maze of little wire cars some with aerials and plastic oranges others with nothing. Nevertheless they would never swap their little cars for any amount of sophisticated metal dinkies. (Once the piccaninny on the farm did make Willy one of their cars in exchange for a number of shirts, which my mother never got to know about until we were back at home.) The day the white children's bus passed through their village would almost certainly be a day to be recorded by the elders. Anyone born on that day in the Ndanga Tribal Trust land would have their birthday remembered with more significance.

In Rhodesia, we sat our main General Certificate of Education (GCE) examinations in November, resitting the following June. It was October 1967 and Willy was going to be sixteen. Adam was going through a period where he felt he had done sufficient for Willy. He said it was time Willy paid his own way. Shortly after his birthday, Willy was taken out of school before even being given the opportunity of writing any examinations. By this time, we had moved once again and now lived just outside of Triangle. Adam had changed his job again. He now worked for the Ministry of Roads, The Roads Department as it was called by the locals. The Roads Department had a very small housing estate made up of prefabricated tin and asbestos rondavel type houses.

Our housing complex was very close to the Mtilikwe River. A hippo made a thorough nuisance of himself while we lived there, returning night after night to uproot all our carrots, eating just the young tender red carrots, and leaving us with the green tops. It was a tremendous joke when one night we heard our uninvited guest grunting and barking in a very deep bass voice plodding through our garden. I ran and locked the back door. Willy said, "I know that guy is intelligent, to find the open gate but I don't think he has mastered the kitchen door yet!" Our rondavel saw the turning of the tide and sad events too.

Adam, after taking Willy out of school, managed to get him on to the work force of the Roads Department. Willy was initially and justifiably employed as an extra worker. Once he began to work, his high grades throughout his schooling in chemistry were soon noted. Diverting to the more technical side, Willy began his training as a Materials Laboratory Technician, affectionately known as a Mud Doctor by the rest of the work force.

The Ministry of Roads were originally to tar the road from Chiredzi to Ngundu Halt, following the original road which passed over the Mtilikwe and Tokwe Rivers. The engineers had for some reason not completed the high level bridges over the Tokwe River. While my mother and little ones, Willy, and I stayed in Triangle, Adam and his work gang were transferred to the Kyle and Zimbabwe Ruins area, where he first encountered Ossie Bristow.

Mr. Bristow in 1968 owned the animal sanctuary Le Rhone. Most of his animals were abandoned pets which included lions, night apes, and monkeys. The animal farm was not far from the main road, and Adam had promised to tar part of his drive. Adam drove the tar-laying machine. Favours such as these would go on all the time. The Kyle to Fort Victoria road was to be nine foot tarmac. With the anticipation of making the road wider later on, the bush was cleared some three foot either side of the nine foot tarred section.

The Africans were all standing on the soft hot dusty side path. Suddenly, there was a rustling, followed by a loud warning roar. A very tired and weary lion emerged shyly. All the Africans scattered in both directions of the road staying on the soft cleared path, only the lion was unaware of the dangers of the black hot sticky tar. The machine was fortunately only four foot wide so only one half of the road was tarred at a time. The lion appeared to be grateful for the respect which resounded in the African's voices as they shouted, "Shumba (lion) Mi whe, Shumba Bass! Shumbai" Gaining confidence because of the speed in which the Africans moved out of his way, he strolled across their path. Ignoring the terrified and hysterical screaming Africans, the lion put his forepaw on to the newly laid tar. An agonising loud roar stopped the Africans in their tracks; instinctively they turned, not wanting to miss any drama, only to find the lion lying down next to the road licking his paw. Adam realising the lion was tamer than most, sent one of his Africans hurtling off on his bicycle to Mr. Bristow's house, who returned almost immediately with a Land Rover. The lion belonged to him and had gone missing that morning. He had broken loose when the vet had tried to give him an injection.

Although I can't say for sure what temperature the tar was, as tar has no specific boiling point, the lion had lost all the hard skin from his paw, and once again, the vet had to be called to attend to the lion, this time to bandage his foot.

While we lived in Triangle, I was fortunate enough to still be able to go to Fort Victoria High School and by now, in my second term, having survived, thankfully, my suicide attempt in my first year (thirteen years old) my very small world was beginning to fall apart. I found school very hard work and bit my nails to the quick. It was not until I went to boarding school that I seriously began to question and realise what was happening to Willy and me was not in any way normal. I began to reflect over the past years.

The one Christmas that Betty came to stay with us in Wankie, it was the first time I never got beaten. It was the same year Willy and I had had our tonsils out. Willy, I am afraid was not so lucky. Adam hit him so badly that he stripped the skin off his back and backside. My mother received her usual punishment for whatever his reason was.

Betty and I sat terrified in my room, which was just across the hallway from Willy's room. Betty started to scream, I begged her to please be very quiet, he might forget we were there and we would not get hit. Betty was shaking as I held my hand over her mouth pleading for her to please be quiet. He never did hit either of us that year and Betty never came to stay with us again on her own.

I looked through the chink in the door one day when my mother was tending to my brother's wounds in the semi dark room. My mother poured glycerin and borax over his back and backside as the skin wept watery blisters like a severe case of nappy rash on a baby's soft tender skin. My eyes began to well over with guilt, had I taken some of his anger, perhaps he would not have hit my brother so badly. Why did Betty have to come, what purpose did she serve, we did not have a good Christmas? The table might have been the best laid out one I had ever seen in our house, but we still got bashed. I felt sure she never went home and told Ouma and Oupa Theron. The beatings never stopped. For me as I have got older to say nothing about something you know is wrong is to condone this behaviour.

My mother mended her glasses frames. Seeing her with mended frames was as common as seeing her wear glasses. I can always remember being a little more outspoken at times. Other times I did not mean to say things out aloud but they sort of just came out aloud. My mother's own father remarried and his wife had come to visit just after this incident with Willy. I said, "Shame Mommy did you drop your glasses again." I knew she did not but I so wanted someone to help us. Why did no one help us, were we so bad, what had to happen to us before people saw that Willy and I needed help? I was told to go and play. There were low whispers. Then I saw this lady go into Willy's room. She came out and said to my mother do you want to get rid of that bastard, just take that kid to the doctor, he will be in jail so fast his head would spin. In my mind, I pleaded please take Willy to the doctor, Mommy, please, we will be rid of him for good. Please take him to the doctor. My mother never did. I never understood the reason for many years. I sometimes wished my stepfather would hit me that badly I would go to the doctor. I was so sure I would. I was convinced I would.

I began to recall the many times before he would come home that my mother would have a sort of premonition that things were not going to go well and would tell Willy and me where we had to meet each other and if one of us arrived there first we just had to wait out of sight until the others arrived. I am not sure why or how this communication broke down one night. We lived in Westgate in the first of the two houses. Quite near the house was a red public telephone booth and a council park; this was our meeting place. Willy and I got thrown out the house the time was not of any consequence, it was dark and we just ran. We waited for what seemed like forever. Adam's car drove past several times. Willy and I lay on the floor until the headlights moved on. Willy said he was sure Adam must have killed my mother or she was so badly hurt she could not get to us so we walked to my Ouma's house. I lost track of the distance. The dark scared me and just so that I knew Willy was with me I talked incessantly. Willy never once said, "Oh just shut up will you." He always answered my every question. We never spoke of Adam or why my mother had not met us, it was general talk. Then without warning, Willy's voice never came back to me like the comforting echo which I was used to. Absolute panic! Where was my brother? How will I find my way to Ouma's house? I started to scream and sob all in the same motion. Please, Willy, please where are you. I heard a quietly muffled voice, 'Myrna, quiet, don't scream, Theron will hear you.' We never called him by his name whenever we referred to him in our own company still to this day we refer to him as Theron. The next thing, there were some Africans standing holding my arms. They were a work gang that were laying a sewerage pipe. Willy had fallen into the deep hole. The Africans helped him out. One asked us why we were out in the dark and where were we going to. I am not sure where in the order of things this man was but he told Willy where we were going was too far for children to walk. He picked me up and put me on his shoulder and took us to Ouma Benadie's house. My mother came there later that morning and Ouma Benadie told her this had to stop. What did she want to happen before she said no more? Adam came a few days later. So many promises were made he said sorry to Willy and said it would never happen again.

I remember twice him joining the AA, but it never worked for him. His temper was just not controllable with or without the drink. As we moved, nothing changed for us. Each house had its own memories of beatings and "get out of my fucking house, this is my house not yours!" Despite this, there were the times when I thought this time for sure it will be different. This time someone will help.

In the Pisa, Adam made me lay in his bed with him. He had thrown my mother and brother out because he had come home and his dinner was too hot for him to eat. The dinner had to be cleaned up off the roughly finished walls a few days after, before we received a visit from Social Welfare. Once Adam was asleep, I made good my escape too and went the short distance to Ouma Benadie's house. I told my mother Adam had tried to have sex with me. She said that he was too drunk to know what he was doing and to forget it. She did tell an Auntie because one night her husband took me home but first called into the pub and on the way home pulled into a lonely dark spot off the main road. He tried his hand and I fought him off. The incident ended with us agreeing never to mention it as he rationalised his behaviour with "I only wanted to see if it was true what they had said about you." What could possibly have been said about a ten-year-old which would make another grownup behave in this manner? Still today it defies my logic. I gave Willy the hedgehog we found. It was a topic for show and tell one day at Newmensford School.

Ouma Benadie had a friend. In those days, we still had the local policeman who walked the beat. He often called in and had the odd cuppa on his rounds. Often joking that he should really be getting out there and catch some villain but was always persuaded to have just another coffee. I happened to turn up to her house just before he arrived. My Ouma had managed to get me settled on a mattress on the floor when she opened the bedroom door and she brought him into the room. In a very soft voice she said, "I am so scared for these kids. One day he is going to kill one of them. Someone has to do something." The policeman did not stay for his cuppa but left straight away. My mother and brother arrived sometime in the night. I remember my mother and Ouma Benadie having an argument. Ouma said, "Well, leave Myrna here now she is sleeping. I will send her home in the morning." Sometime later we had a visit from Social Welfare and both my parents told lies. They told them that the incident the other night was a one off, it never happened on a regular basis. Willy and I stood in the kitchen. I remember asking Willy why they do not ask the children, "I would tell them I would tell them everything." Willy said, "No, you would not!" He stormed out of the kitchen. He was right, I told them nothing. I meekly took in the tea tray when called like an obedient dog follows his master to the grave.

Try as I might I was always in trouble. Adam had thrown me across the kitchen floor for going swimming one day when the previous week when I asked I was told "No!" My head hit the sink. I can so clearly remember thinking, why did you go swimming Myrna and then as if to rationalise it I told myself how was I to know last week's no meant no forever and the rest of my life. Adam told me to get to my room, he was not finished with me yet. If I thought the blood on my head was the only blood I was going to see, I was to think again. As he furiously walked past the dining room table, he savagely picked up a chair and threw it out of his way. This time, I was not going to meekly walk after him like that obedient dog. I ran out the double French doors. I ran out on to the road caught up with my mother and the three kids. Grabbed Gretha and ran into the sugar cane field. I would be safe there, he would not be able to follow us into the cane field. Gretha and I would be safe. He caught up with my mother told her to get home with his fucking kids and where was that other fucking bitch? Where had she taken his kid? Gretha and I just ran blindly for sometime I could see his torch looking for us. In the middle of the cane fields, I came across a small tin shanty village. The Africans gave us shelter for a while but I could still hear him shouting and looking for us. The Africans tried to tell me he would not find us but I had to keep going. Gretha and I walked the entire night through the cane fields. I saw a cane rat for the very first time, they were as big as cats as some had described them to us. I had wet my pants I was too scared to stop. Gretha got very tired and I carried her on my shoulders. I was lost. I could not find a way out of the cane field. Willy, where are you? I prayed quietly in my mind you would find a way out. It was as if he really was looking out for me. Something told me to look for a landmark and head for it. I saw for the first time the guesthouse's lights.

The guesthouse was a house that the Hippo Valley Estate put visiting guests in when they came on business to the Lowveld. The light was so bright though that when I looked away it was so dark it was difficult to adjust my eyes to the dark. I walked towards the light and eventually came out of the cane fields. Gretha and I went to a church minister's house. I stayed there for four days and would not go home. The police came and talked to me. They told me that Adam was so drunk he had passed out on the floor and had not hurt the other children. They told me people can get that drunk they don't even remember what they have done and this was the case with Adam. My mother told me not to make a scene and to come home immediately. She said Adam had said he was sorry if he had done anything to hurt me. I told her he always says that we go back home and it starts all over again. I did go back home and had to clean the bantam rooster's blood off the wall. Adam had killed our pet bantam, pulled its head off and left him to spray his blood over the kitchen walls. Adam told me the rooster was dead because I did not take my punishment and when he says no next time I will remember it means no until he says otherwise. I thought about this at the time and thought ha, those cops tried to tell me he does not remember what he did. What idiots are they? Again no one seemed to be able to help. My mother told Willy and me when we lived in Ndola not to upset Adam, as he had been the perfect father and husband while we were with her sister. Willy said, "Well, then why don't you leave us with Auntie Muriel." He was told not to be cheeky and just watch himself.

I was always very protective of Gretha. As I child I did not understand why this was, but as I got older I thought perhaps it had something to do with the time my mom went into hospital to have Ockert. Adam took me out of school (I would have turned ten earlier in the year) to look after him and the other children. I know now from research children who are given adult responsibilities at a very early age cannot let go of these responsibilities. Now psychologists have a name for it Parentification. Gretha was always a very poor eater. I was ten by the time Ockert was born. I was sure just as I would eat when I got hungry so too would Gretha. I never force-fed her like my mother did. Gretha was regularly wrapped tightly in a bath towel with her hands firmly tucked in, spoonful after spoonful was shovelled down her mouth. If she got sick and vomited she just got more of the same, with a good sharp slap and as she cried so more food was pushed in her mouth. My mother was in hospital for three days. Adam went to collect her; he had to sign a release form as my mother was very ill after the birth of Ockert. Women were still regarded a man's property even though they had the vote. He would not sign a certificate for her to have a total hysterectomy because he was of the belief that once women had that done she no longer wanted sex. His life revolved around sex. He told my mother I had tried to kill one of his kids. Gretha went to hospital suffering from malnutrition. My mother asked what was I trying to do, why had I not fed Gretha? I was silent, why did I not feed her, was it because I was just too lazy, as Adam had said? I really did think she would eat and drink when she got hungry. She was only a little tot of three.

When I tried to kill myself, I think I really didn't want to die but I was always in so much trouble. I remember being very scared and wondering if I died would I go to hell and how bad would it be. I thought when one has a dog that is untrainable and an absolute menace, never doing what it's told, a dog that one cannot even train not to do the basic things, 'like not pee on the carpet,' one takes it to the vet and has it put down. I have known people to have pets put down because they simply do not fit into their lifestyle any more. One should be able to do that to kids. Why were we any different to a dog or other pet? If Adam was in a room and I happened to walk into it, I would make every excuse under the sun to get out of the room because I knew I would be in trouble for something. As kids we were never allowed to go out of the yard. I got a hiding once because I cut my finger in a hand mincer while forcing the meat down the funnel and turning the handle at the same time. I went next door to ask for a Band-Aid. I took the top of one of my fingers off and still have the scar (Band-Aid incident 1965, scar still visible 1985). I told Willy when he came home from school about it he said, "You know the deal, you are not allowed out the yard." Willy had to be right, had he not looked out for me all these past years. I was just plain naughty untrainable an absolute menace. Adam told me I was so useless I would not even make a good fucking useless housewife. I can remember thinking when I woke up after taking the pills. He has to be right I can't even get this right, how useless am I?

Something inside of me was changing. I wanted to be loved. I too, wanted to be proud of my home life, like the other girls at school, to talk affectionately of my parents but that was not possible as I was sure they never loved me or regarded me with any affection.

My last visit to the farm Adam had never bothered me before while I was there. I am not sure why this time was different. He said to go for a walk with him. That inner little voice which kids have and is so often right told me to take Betty with me. I begged her but she had her own reasons and never came with me.

Walking along the same leafy pine tree lane that had brought us to Eenheid, Adam tried to get me to have sex with him. I just playfully ran between the trees. Adam got more and more angry as I just played the fool. Eventually he said, "Get home!"

I needed to tell someone of my hurt. I am not sure if this was the reason at the time but as I have got older I have observed that if people are really hurting and feel for whatever reason another has something to do with that pain they say and do things to, if you like, even the score. Perhaps Betty not coming with me I wanted to even the score. I told her about the pain I had been hiding since I was nine years old. I had tried to talk to my mother but she never quite had the same concern about my problem as I did. I found it very hard, when at first I thought of Adam as her father. Once I started to tell her, one event led to another. Betty never once said, "I don't believe you" or

"You must be exaggerating." She was able to talk to Ouma Theron despite the generation gap, she told Ouma of my dilemma.

Adam opened Betty's reply letter to me. We were never allowed to have any mail of our own. He was outraged and completely blinded by his anger. I had, he said, turned his daughter against him with yet another one of my lies. He was so sure that the best thing to do was to lay the blame on me. He felt sure that he could convince my mother it was I who was wrong. Through the threat of being sent to reform school, I stuck my ground. No longer was I going to stay at home. For some days, I was sent to Coventry, even Willy would not talk to me. My mother just said that if I wanted to cause trouble there were other ways of doing it. How lonely and lost I felt. I found out in 2013 Willy was told he was not to speak to me, why no one ever told him.

Everyone still spoke to Adam yet he was in the wrong. I had only spoken out. Things never got better for me at home. Adam at one point realised I was not going to change my story, he admitted that he had a few times tried to make advances towards me but he had assured, or tried to assure, my mother that it was only done in a very playful manner. So often a lie is covered up with half a truth. Adam wrote and apologised to me. (This letter would have to be on file at Fort Victoria where my court case took place.)

For a time, though I was never able to come to terms with everyone at home. Things were almost normal. Adam never talked to me or asked me for anything and my mother hovered over my every move. She could not watch me at boarding school. It was during the time that Adam was at Kyle that he came to the hostel and took me out for the day. Adults unfortunately don't always exercise their authority at the right time. Today I would like to think as we become more aware of the different signs of child abuse, adults would be suspicious if a child is still wetting their bed at fourteen and having tried to previously commit suicide something was seriously wrong. The decision was once again left up to me. Still being very afraid of my stepfather, I went out with him and he took me to his camp site at Kyle where he tried to rape me.

Adam had locked the rondavel's door but I climbed through the small window and ran to the next camp site which was only just out of ear shot of his rondavel. The people asked if my dad was having a lie down I had said yes. When he arrived he said, "Come on, Myrna, best get you back to the hostel." I threatened I would tell the whole camp if he did not take me back immediately with that I got into the backseat of the car. I never understood why he did take me back when, I as an adult, realise all the things that could have happened, I consider how fortunate I was that he took me straight back to the hostel. I think so much back to this journey and just have to accept there is some good in everyone.

I told Miss Drinkwater my whole story when I arrived back at the hostel. I also said never again was I ever going home, threatening her with a more successful suicide. She called Social Welfare who in turned said it was not their concern it was a police matter.

At this point in the original draft I wrote a very matter of fact sentence. Following a court case, I was sent to the Rhodesian Childrens' Home— which I immediately put a line through. I felt and still do feel very strongly about the manner in which I was made to think of myself as a criminal. These feelings have had a very lasting effect on me and it is because of these strong feelings that I wanted to include the following paragraphs. I regard it as a silent protest.

I have always held on to the thought that my mother felt a closeness towards me, but she never let me know her feelings. We never spoke to each other about any of what had previously happened. It was only me, the authorities, and Adam. The police women who took my statement never tried to gain my confidence. The only consideration I was shown was when she came to the school to pick me up she was in plain clothes. This was not that much help as one of the head staff recognised her for who she was and said, "So what has this one been up to?" Not surprisingly, I left out large portions of my story. It was only when Adam stated that I was lying and if anyone had been wronged, it was he. I produced the letter that he had written to me the previous year and yet another statement was taken. I was collected from school after lunch, and when I left the police station, the entire building was in darkness as everyone had gone home for the night.

Adam then accused me of being a whore, saying that I had slept with a number of boyfriends. I was most perplexed when I was asked about this by my police lady. How could she ask me something like that? Indeed why would I complain about my stepfather if I was that sort of girl. I was furious, hurt, and humiliated when I found myself in a hospital ward being examined by doctors. Not even the doctors would talk to me. They talked in low whispers glaring at me from time to time. The people were faceless; their eyes showed no emotion. No one would tell me anything or explain why it was all happening.

My day in court was horrific. Through a flood of tears I was asked once again to reveal and relive my past years. The court room only had a few people in it, together with my mother, Adam, and the judge. I had asked the police woman to come with me, but she said she wasn't allowed in court. I had come to respect her and what she represented. During the court session, I lost track of time. At one point, the judge asked Adam if he had anything he wanted to question me on. He said no but he just wanted to ask me if I ever saw him in the street to please acknowledge him. My head ached and my legs were very tired when I walked slowly out of the court room. On my way back to school in the unmarked police car I fell asleep.

My mother came to see me later that day and told me Adam had been sent to prison for a year for attempted rape. When I asked what was to happen to me, she said I was to go home at the end of term. I was so afraid of Adam and felt sure he would kill me if I went home and told my mother this. Auntie Muriel then offered to keep me and though the prospect of living with my favourite aunt appealed to me, I felt that I would not be safe there either. I chose to go to the Rhodesian Childrens' Home in Salisbury.

In 1967, Sarah, a girl who lived in Kamative, was also a boarder at Fort Victoria, was writing a letter to a friend. When she finished, she put it in the envelope and asked me to post it along with my mail. Just as

I slipped it into the post box the name caught my eye, M.D. Looij. I asked Sarah when next she wrote to her friend to enquire if he knew Myrna and Willy Looij. Sarah's friend turned out to be my very own father.

My father arrived unannounced one evening at the hostel. I was totally unprepared for him. I was told by Miss Drinkwater, the superintendent, that a man claiming to be my father had arrived and wanted to see me. She said that I needn't see him if I didn't want to. I was very bewildered by this remark and thought, "Why on earth would I not want to see my own father?"

I met my dad in the matron's staff room and though I wanted to tell him I was glad I had a father and that I hoped he loved me, all I was able to talk to him about was Willy, how very ill he had been over the years and how, despite missing a whole year of school he was still very clever and was working now. When my dad left, I went back to the dormitory not being able to face any of the other girls. I lay on my bed and sobbed pathetically. I could not understand why I was crying nor did I want to stop. I cried till my eyes ached and I felt sick. I never heard the other girls coming in from prep and it suited me when they all thought Miss Drinkwater had upset me, for how was I to explain to someone else something for which I myself had no explanation. Meeting my father held no movie romance.

I remember after my court case, I had returned to school. I carried on with my studies as though it was just another day in the park. No fuss, no counselling. It was as though nothing extraordinary had happened with one exception. My father arrived a few days later at the hostel. He was with my mother not sure how this was arranged but he wanted to take custody of me. I remember thinking how would this ever work? He was an electrician on a mine. He lived in men's single quarters. Where and how would I fit into his world? I was left to make a very adult choice and said, "No, I will just go to the Home." I was made a ward of the state until I was 21.

Once Adam was behind bars, Willy seized the opportunity too and left home going to South Africa. Willy finally said he knew why he was made to get rid of the flea beaten Alsatian. That animal was as smart as any Siamese cat. He had seen the reaction this dog had towards Adam. Siamese cats, no matter where my stepfather encountered them they would not abide him. Not for any price would this breed of cat tolerate him. They would hiss and snarl hunching their backs angrily at him. Adam only once, did he ever try and make friends with one and boy did he get the fright of his life. The only other time I have known Adam to appear lost for words was the one and only time my mother hit him back with a solid square sable ashtray. Cut Adam above his eyebrow. I seem to remember the beating stopped after that. I have always maintained from a very early age the only way to put a stop to a bully is to stand up to them. My mother and the three little ones went to live in Gwelo with her sister, Auntie Muriel. My mother's last request to me was that I should never say that she sent me away. That was true. It was my choice from all the choices the adults around me were presenting me with, I feel it was my only choice. Despite her request we drifted apart only occasionally writing to one another. I can't remember ever getting a card on my birthday or a Christmas card while I was in the Childrens' Home; I was forgotten and totally alone now.

Before saying my final good-bye to the Lowveld, forgive me if I reminisce on a place that had been my home for the longest, at any one time, in my short little life. Looking back, the many happy days spent swimming in the smaller subsidiary canals come, first to mind. Splashing loudly, with shrieks of laughter, as one child warned another of the current taking them closer and closer to the small outlets leading into the small and many man-made dams. We would shriek with trepidation as we imagined going down the plug hole with the bathwater. Sometimes they dared the current to do just that, by floating or just simply lifting their feet off the canal bottom. The water would then be pumped out into numerous overhead sprinklers bringing the most vital commodity to the sugar plantations.

Looking far into the setting sun an even green carpet could be seen, broken only by the odd baobab tree as it stood, thickly set, emerging from the tall green cane. The solitary tree looked stark and mysterious but there was no mistaking its purpose. When the sugar cane was ripe, the long green pampas type foliage was burnt, leaving slightly charred canes. The baobab was the look-out tower. The fire spread furiously, leaping from one plant to its very close neighbour, till the air was thick with blue grey smoke and small black specks flickered and jumped in the air like small 'speed-boat' insects skating across the pond's surface. Scampering from the heat into the next sugar cane field were the cane rats.

The fire was soon replaced by gangs of Africans armed with large 'pangas' (very big knives) who slashed the cane off close to the ground, laying the cane in large bundles for the crane operator. All this work was carried out by African staff. The cane was loaded into high loading trailers, thousands of sticks at a time, they were then taken to the sugar mill to be crushed and made into sugar.

To think that I and people like me owe it all to one solitary man, who made this otherwise barren sunbaked hostile part of Rhodesia more liveable. It is thanks to Murray Mac Dougall that I spent, basically, a very happy four years in the Lowveld and it is with kind permission from the author, Colin Saunders, of "Murray Mac Dougall and the Story of Triangle, an Epic of Land, Water and Man" that I am able to pass on and perhaps clear up a few misunderstandings about this very impressive pioneer as most pioneers are.

Thomas Murray Mac Dougall was born on the 4 March 1881 on the farm Auchnashelloch on Loch Awe, Argyllshire, Scotland. At fourteen years old, Mac Dougall, because of a severe recession, left school and worked as a general hand in a shipbuilding yard. While at Cammell, Laird and Co., Mac Dougall secured a practical expertise and love for mechanical things. It was here that he met fascinating people and while he listened intently to their stories of visited lands, his unquenchable thirst for travel and adventure grew. Leaving Scotland he joined a cattle-boat and sailed with it to Argentina.

In 1898, after working his way through some South American countries, including Brazil, he served in President Castro's army in Venezuela. In Guyana, he worked in sugar-cane fields at Demerara. Some people get the notion that it was because of his work at Demerara that he grew sugar in Triangle. This is not true at all. The Guyana fields were in swamps and needed to be drained, Triangle needed water brought to the fields.

Mac Dougall made his way to South Africa when he managed to get a working passage on a ship in 1902. At Cape Town, he enlisted in the South African Constabulary and was to fight for the British in the Boer War but the war ended before he was sent out into the field. He then worked for a cartage firm, displaying his natural talents to command a wagon and team of animals, which stood him in good stead during a later war. During the slack periods in his job, he trekked into the wild bush on horseback. It was just such a time when he travelled north crossing the Limpopo where he reached the Mtilikwe River, Mac Dougall spent a few weeks here, making friends with a few Shangaans (a tribe of Africans from the Lowveld). He had fallen in love with this corner of Rhodesia just as Livingstone had, when he saw the Victoria Falls for the first time when he remarked: "It has never been seen before by European eyes——but scenes so lovely must have been gazed upon by angels in their flight." Mac Dougall was also spellbound by the wilderness of this unexplored, almost uninhabited, fascinatingly strange, part of Rhodesia and so vowed to return one day.

In 1908, after undertaking a number of tasks, he made his way to Salisbury where he lived for four years. In his party was a piccaninny from Swaziland, Tom Dunaza, six Europeans, a coloured man, and nine African men. A severe famine in 1912 had a firm grip and the government appealed for help to relieve the desperate and starving people of the Victoria district. Mac Dougall and Tom ferried grain on their animal drawn wagons to the Bikita and Zaka regions. Mac Dougall revisited the Lowveld and still he had the same strong feelings about the Lower Mtilikwe region. He returned to Salisbury and applied for rights to three hundred thousand acres of land between the Mtilikwe, Chiredzi, and Lundi Rivers. Because this region had never been surveyed, there was a lengthy delay before his grant was given. He was given the option to buy. Unfortunately before he was able to do anything with the land, the First World War broke out. Mac Dougall returned to England to fight for king and country in the First King Edward's Horses, where he was awarded the Military Cross. Tom moved away and looked for work elsewhere.

Returning to Cape Town in 1919, Mac Dougall found that the raging 'flu epidemic had severely hit District Six. (District Six is a slum area on the outskirts of Cape Town. In 1975, I passed through this area. Though most of it had been demolished, it still bore horrific remains.) Disregarding his own safety, Mac Dougall rallied to their assistance. After removing the dead bodies, his payment was a case of Scotch whisky. This was his only request. Mac Dougall eventually arrived back in Salisbury, having secured his grant with the directors of the British South Africa Company. (He had on a previous visit found that his land had been offered to someone else.) Salisbury processed his rights of option to purchase the land which is today known as Triangle, Buffalo Range, and Hippo Valley, for four pence an acre. Mac Dougall had always dreamed of a cattle ranch, so after forming a partnership with Mark Spraggen, they bought lock, stock, and barrel from a farmer, named Van Niekerk, who was going out of business. Mac Dougall and partner named their ranch Triangle and it was a good coincidence: their cattle already displayed a triangle shaped brand.

Tom, hearing through a very efficient bush telegraph that his good friend was back, travelled day and night to appear one day, unexpectedly, while Mac Dougall was building himself a home. Tom greeted Mac Dougall with "Master, I have come." Mac Dougall gladly welcomed him and Tom was made supervisor over many tasks. Mac Dougall is portrayed as a unique pioneer in that he never set out to achieve personal gain or wealth. He seems to have been able to work with his fellow men. Often, on returning to the Lowveld, he would bring a wagon load of Mealie Meal (Maize meal) back with him because he knew that this is what the people needed most.

Cattle prices fell, due to the post war depression and Mac Dougall's ranching enterprise was short lived. By 1922, he was forced to sell most of his stock and his partnership with Mark Spraggen was dissolved. Mac Dougall wasn't a beaten man. He turned his attentions to a project which was to be the birth of a new world. He had to get water to his rich, sandy soil. This water would have to come from the Mtilikwe River.

In 1923, his scheme was surveyed by a government engineer, who travelled from Fort Victoria by mule cart. When Mac Dougall tried to dig foundations he only hit sandy soil, so he moved the weir site upstream and the Jutala Weir was built. This new site posed a problem, two large granite kopjies (small hills) stood right in the path of his proposed canal. The ever resourceful Scot was not to be discouraged. Mac Dougall displayed his will power, against all odds, he and a handful of Shangaans chopped with picks and shovels for seven years. They were only able to work for six months out of the year as during the rainy season their tunnels flooded. Mac Dougall plotted, with uncanny accuracy, with the help of a rifle's sights, where the entrance and exit would be in the large solid rock hills. The two tunnels are one thousand, four hundred foot long followed by an eight mile canal. Triangle's pioneering irrigation masterpiece is now a National Monument and has a simple bronze plaque which reads:

From this weir's, built in 1923, Thomas Murray Mac Dougall led water from the Mtilikwe River through two tunnels, hewn by hand over seven years, a distance of 1400 feet through solid rock, and thence to his lands through a canal eight miles long. This historic enterprise was the first development in the Lowveld's great irrigation project

With an adequate supply of water to his land Mac Dougall planted a variety of crops. The quelea (a small gregarious species of finch) did his harvesting for him. They stripped his entire crop. The red locusts then ate, without showing any mercy, the remaining crops. Mac Dougall then turned his attentions to sugar cane. In 1934, he applied to the government to import a load of seed-cane from Natal. His application was regarded with contempt and perhaps it was only due to his faithful friend C.L. Robertson, who was the Director of Irrigation, that he was granted permission to import only three lengths of cane. (Whether these were the lengths which were put into the ground or the lengths that were cut at harvest time I am not sure, but either way we are talking of a very small allowance. The difference between these two lengths being that one is about three foot long and the other eight to ten foot long.)

Mac Dougall imported his three lengths and more besides. Mac Dougall realized that nothing, or very little, could be gained from a meagre three lengths, decided not to declare when he arrived at the border post at Beit Bridge, the cane which he had strapped to the undercarriage of his motor car. At a later date, he drove an even larger lorry load of cane through a section of the Limpopo River. During the winter, sections of this massive river are often dry.

Unlike the government, he was so very sure that he would succeed he bought a mill which would help him manufacture his first harvest. The huge monstrosity had to be transported by road from the railway siding at Beit Bridge. The very same road that we used in 1965 to get from Ngunda Halt to Chiredzi was mapped out and built by Mac Dougall so that he could transport his dismantled mill. The many different rivers that he had to cross were often raging torrents, flooded by the good seasonal rains Mac Dougall unloaded his mill and drove home, intending to return weeks later. The landscape had changed so dramatically with the phenomenal rate at which the bush had grown; he could not find his mill. The next time Mac Dougall encountered a swollen river he put his own land mark on the larger trees, now he need not wait until the winter set in and killed the undergrowth before he was able to recover his mill.

However, these facts have only recently come to my knowledge. I grew up during a period where parents were to be obeyed. Children were regarded more like possessions. As one puts a chair in a room, children had their place. Adults, in general, were right without question, so it's little wonder, the people that were our pioneers had to be portrayed as upstanding, law abiding citizens. This point of fact is no pardon and facts are facts and should always be told as such.

As a child, in our history lesson we were told a very sad and touching tale, which roused sympathy from the hardest of hearts. How we wished that Mac Dougall had been rich and some even thought if only he owned shares in the railways, it would have been an asset. "Mac Dougall had imported a load of seed-cane but when it arrived in the Lowveld, because of the very long way it had to come and transport being so unreliable, it had all rotted, except for three pieces. Mac Dougall, being a true pioneer, planted his three lengths."

"Worse disaster was to follow. After purchasing a mill in Natal it had to be transported piece by piece in his old truck. His old truck, not having his heart of steel and will to keep going, broke down under the strain of the huge pieces of metal; it was beyond repair. The mill was then transported by ox-wagon and it took this ever inventive pioneer two years to get his mill erected."

Finally on September 11, 1939, the entire mill recovered and erected, his sister, who visited him from Britain each Rhodesian Summer, opened his mill. She was later killed during the London blitz. From Mac Dougall's initial forty-five acres he proudly drove down to the refinery in Bulawayo, his first ninety-six tons of raw sugar. Mac Dougall was ecstatic he had proved his point. Though Mac Dougall is not entirely above reproach in his manner of achieving his aim the Lowveld has never looked back, it continues to be a thriving part of Rhodesia. To quote a very old cliché: 'Where there is a will, there is a way.' Thanks to Thomas Murray Mac Dougall, we lesser mortals were shown the way.

Bob Klette Myrna

Christmas England 1980

Kids_1965

Kids_Chiredzi_1965

Mark Allan Backwoods Cooking England

Mark and Allan LonePine 1990

Marriage Theron

Myrna and Mrs Gus Foster Mom

Myrna Keith at Kentucky Hotel

Myrna 50th 2003

Myrna 1969

Seagrave Farewell England 1989

The Cake

The Register

Theron Kids 1967

Will FortVic 1966

The Rhodesian Childrens Home

At the end of term, Adam was still in jail, I spent a few weeks with my mother in Gwelo. Our time was very short and we never talked about the sad events. This was to remain an unspoken event all her life. I gave my mother a small gold plated carriage clock as a going away present. It made her very sad and heartsore. I never understood this. I thought she should feel as I did. I was proud of my gift. It was the first present that I had given her, and it was bought with my own money.

Just before I left Gwelo, I was described to Mrs Whittle, at the Rhodesian Childrens Home, during a phone call, as a "rather plump girl with mousy brown hair and blue eyes." Within the same week, I found myself on the overnight train, with strict instructions to wait under the large clock on the platform at Salisbury Station.

On my arrival, to my horror, there was not one large clock on the platform but three! Walking along the platform like a lost country mouse visiting his town friend, I was just beginning to panic when a lady came up to me. "Are you Myrna Looij?" she said. "Yes, I am," I replied. Then, really wanting her to understand why I was not standing where I was told to stand, I tried to explain about the clocks. Mrs. Whittle never took the slightest notice, interrupted me saying, "My car is this way."

The Rhodesian Children's Home is in Eastlea, a suburb of Salisbury. It was started in 1918, mainly because of the same Spanish influenza epidemic that hit District Six. Mr. Rosin's father, who was a rabbi, saw the need for a home for children who had lost their parents during this epidemic. He went out and collected, personally, the many homeless children, in much the same way as Dr. Barnardo did. Mr. Rosin Junior was still actively involved in the Home, and one of the more modern houses was named after his mother. It's called Muriel Rosin.

The Home has a wonderful set up. Instead of one large hostel, there are five houses, two very big semi-detached buildings. Downstairs we had a locker room with basins and toilets and a small kitchen with a small amount of utensils, a kettle and small cooker. The matron's sewing room was next to the kitchen. Walking from the small entrance hall, one walked into a large room. This was the little one's playroom. In the one corner was a neatly painted dolls' house with pretty lace curtains and remnants of the larger house's curtains. Large toys and a big table to play table tennis on, when it was not in use it doubled as a homework table.

Closing off the older girls' sitting room from the little ones room was a concertina type door. A large bookcase covered half of the outermost wall, continuing along the length of the other outside wall. The wall on the opposite short side of the room had a very big window and mounted below that was an electric fire. Our sitting room was finished off with a square rug and odd, though comfortable, chairs. Our house shared a TV which was in this room, but in our sister house. Auntie Bessie was the matron of that house. Upstairs was the large bathroom with partitioned off toilets and baths as well as two showers and four hand basins. Next to that, above our sitting room, was the nine to twelve-year-old girls' bedroom. Above the children's playroom was another bedroom for the little, six to nine year olds. Very close to this room on the opposite side of the hallway was our matron. Miss Napier's room led out through French doors on to an adjoining balcony with Auntie Bessie. Immediately opposite her door and above the kitchen and sewing room was my bedroom. There were only four senior girls in the Home while I was there and we paired off into these rooms. There was an inter-leading door joining the two houses upstairs.

When Mrs. Whittle retired because of her husband's ill health, shortly after I arrived, Mrs. Tilbrook took over her post. Some changes were immediately noticeable like the sign on her door changed from Matron in Charge to Superintendent. Something which she also tried to bring about was to have the younger boys time extended before they were transferred to St. Joseph's Boys Home, but while I was there, this had not come about. They were still sent at nine. Mrs. Tilbrook felt that nine was too young for some boys to be taken away from a woman's influence and placed in an all-male run home. Also we had so few boys of this age, it often meant that only one or two boys went away at any one time. The other point which was raised was that at thirteen, all children went up to high school which usually meant a new school. Being transferred at nine meant breaking into their education more than was necessary. This added to the strain on these very young children.

The main building housed the superintendent's flat upstairs and a number of different flats and rooms. Downstairs the main foyer led into the staff dining room and the very large children's dining room, with the secretary's and superintendent's office in the foreground. The main kitchen was behind the two dining rooms.

Looking out of the dining room windows, one could see the caretaker's flat and the very large rose garden inside the horseshoe shape which the kitchen, dining room, and flat made. The flatlet was attached to the kitchen end of Muriel Rosin House, giving the owners their own private front door, garage, and gateway.

We reached Muriel Rosin through inter leading doors from the dining room. This house was, when it was first built, the nursery but later a larger building was built behind the hall and quite separate from the main buildings, mainly because of the noise. Muriel Rosin was now used for a storeroom because there were too few children. The library and senior girls' study was also housed here.

Whenever I think of the Home, our study room becomes a living image. I remember each chair, the pictures on the wall, the large table, at which I sat doing hours of homework, the selection of books and encyclopaedia. I loved that room and felt very safe in it. When I bought my first set of encyclopaedia, it was the beginnings of a dream. One day, I would duplicate that room in my own home. Paintings which had been created with such pride were hung proudly. My best was a copy of a 'Constable' painted by Daddy Fred, Keith's father. The floor would too be covered in a rich thick pile carpet.

Often I think of my days in the Home and what outsiders called us children—Underprivileged kids. Never, while living there, or since, did I think of myself as someone deprived of any privileges. How privileged is anyone who is allowed to receive their own mail. We were all close to one another. Very often, we found a closeness in some children more than we did in others. This happens, in very large families, children pair off with each other, trusting them and only them, sharing with each other some common bond. We were all privileged and had very caring people around us all the time. These feelings bring to mind Adam's death, which happened in February 1975. Willy said, with pity, how very sorry he was for Betty as now she had no one of her own. I had no feelings of pity for Betty but thought quietly to myself —which is worse, having no parents or having a figurehead that didn't care? I still think the latter cuts a far deeper wound.

Mrs. Tilbrook would invite Sheila, Moira, Sharon, and me to her flat, often, for dinner. At first, I did think it was perhaps because there were only four of us that this happened but Mrs Tilbrook repeated the treat for some of the younger children too. Cooking the meal was done mainly by Mrs. Tilbrook but we all enjoyed the little tasks we were set, retiring later to coffee and a chat. So many different little, unimportant things came out at these dinners. The whole evening was so relaxing and enjoyable. We looked forward to returning for our next meal.

Mrs. Tilbrook enjoyed flowers and liked them about. It later became a weekly task, for those who wanted to do it, to cut fresh flowers from our large and beautiful gardens and arrange them in vases in the main hallway and dining rooms. Certain parts of the garden were regarded as the flower garden. In October, one could sit on park type benches under the shady jacaranda trees when the purple trumpet like flowers fall off the trees, the barren soil under the entire umbrella of the jacaranda tree is covered in a carpet of purple, lilac hue. The little flowers gently pop as you tread and flatten them.

One afternoon, while sitting on one of these benches under the trees, just after a shower of rain, I had a crow's company. He was high up in the branches, catching his feast. The rain had stirred the flying ants (termites). Crawling to their opening in the ground they spread their wings and flew high. Some getting past the jet black evil shadow, most hardly used to their wings, were gulped greedily as he sat stretching out his neck, catching his meal. Then, suddenly, noticing an ant slightly larger, maybe browner than most, he overstretched and fell out of the tree. Thinking it was really going to fall, I shouted, "Fly, you stupid bird!" What a fool, I felt, as if a bird would fall, rather than fly. Hoping against all hope that no one had heard me, I looked around. Then, quickly feeling very self conscious and needing something to distract even me, I picked up a handful of flowers, pretending to examine them closely.

Mrs. Tilbrook was so different to the adults that had gone before in my life. She took time off her work to talk to us. In the afternoons, around three, those who wanted to, which was usually all of us, would go up to our swimming pool. It was larger than most private pools but then most families did not have thirty or forty children. Though our pool was fenced off from the nursery, we could see the smaller boys and girls playing in their sandpits, swings, and paddling pool. The highlight of the afternoon was when Mrs. Tilbrook came up to the pool, bringing along any stray children, who for one reason or another would not come swimming at first. As she opened the gate, we all stopped playing and she was met with screams and shouts of, "Hello, Mrs. Tilbrook, watch me!" Someone else wanted to be noticed. "I can do better than that, watch me." Slowly, she worked her way round and watched us all, giving a few tips and words of encouragement.

Most Sundays, we had visitors. The older boys from St. Joseph's would visit their younger brothers or sisters, friends and relations would also visit. These afternoons passed very quickly for those who had visitors while others chose to stay in their rooms or just indoors. Mrs. Tilbrook often took advantage of this time and visited us. Knocking on our door, she would ask if she might come in. Refusing a chair, she would kick her shoes off and sit with her feet tucked up under her skirt on one of our beds. These little chats took many shapes, from shaving our legs to making our faces up. From why one cream stung more than another to when it was the best time to shave, morning or evening? It was as a result of one such chat that she got a lady to come and speak to us on Saturday morning on makeup and dress sense.

We were encouraged to make use of our tennis courts with a promise from Mrs. Tilbrook to come and watch us. None of us were at all good and that we had let the tennis courts go into disrepair did not help. It was like playing tennis with a rugby ball. You never quite knew where it would bounce once it had hit the ground.

I was never all that good at school but when I brought home my College of Preceptors Certificate results (this an examination between our school leaver's exam at sixteen and GCE O level at seventeen. If one was in a B stream one took five years to O level, unlike the A stream pupils who took four years skipping out COP altogether.) I achieved eight out of ten passes which included two credits and a distinction. It was my best day. I was on cloud nine. I could have whatever I wanted. Mrs. Tilbrook fulfilled her promise of my very own pair of dressmaker's scissors. Strict instructions followed my request—they had to cut right to the point! I remember thinking how silly of Mrs Tilbrook but knowing that that was the most important thing about a good pair of scissors. When she asked, "Is that very important?" "Oh yes!" I replied, and Sharon then said. "Even I know that." I am sure that was only because I was always saying so.

At Christmas time, we were asked to write to Father Christmas. So as to encourage the younger children, we all sat down one afternoon and wrote our letters. Sheila wrote once, "Dear Mother Christmas, please may I have a Rolls Royce." Mrs. Tilbrook bought her a little Rolls Royce dinky, a bright shining gold one.

As it was Christmas time when I first arrived at the Home, there were very few children about. I was taken upstairs to my room and shown where I could unpack my clothes. A large part of the house closes down over the school holidays. Only the very young children in the nursery are looked after. Some children go home to one-parent families or other relations but most of us had foster homes. My foster parents were coming to collect me after lunch.

Mr. and Mrs. Blank arrived as planned and we all went shopping. They had six of their own children and five 'Home' children. I felt so strange, everyone knew everyone else, I was the odd one out. For the first time, I thought to myself what have I let myself in for, why could I just not stay at the Home? Then Mrs Blank noticed me wandering further away from the other children and tried to bridge the gap between us. She explained that each child was to be given five dollars to buy our Christmas presents. I don't remember what our money was spent on but the afternoon soon passed and we were on our way to their farm at Umvukwes.

The Blanks had a very large tobacco farm and once there I felt quite at home. Tobacco was something I knew about and told everyone of my Ouma's and Oupa's biggest tobacco farm in the whole world. It was at this farm though that I saw the different stages that tobacco go through while being processed. At Eenheid, I saw it being picked and hung but we were never around when the crop was graded in the field which ultimately affected the overall price one received at the tobacco auctions. Mr. Blank started to take a serious interest in one particular farm as he became aware that this neighbouring farmer's tobacco bails always fetched a very much higher price on the floor than his and whom he felt had a much poorer crop in the field. He worked out that certain farmers either had the inspectors over for an early morning breakfast followed by the grading or would invite them for a Braai the night before put them up for the night and then have their fields graded in the morning. Mrs. Blank was put to work in the kitchen, the inspector was given the best morning or afternoon tea fit for a king, and then the fields were graded. At this stage, the crop was graded on how weed free the entire crop was the soil condition and the overall size of the plant. The tobacco was graded a second time once it was dried and before it was bailed. Each lot was given a tag with an official stamp on it a lot number and then auctioned off at the Tobacco Auctions. The tags were to set the starting price for each lot. The auctions were once open to all, but as time went on and more backhanded deals were being made, it became a closed shop and farmers were only given what they were told was the price their tobacco fetched and there was no proof of anything else.

The Blank farm did cater more for a family. They had a very big house with a large swimming pool. We all had fantastic fun till one day I was thrown into the pool with all my clothes on. I had then to confess to Auntie Trina that I only had one bra. She asked me if I had just forgotten to pack more than one but I told her I only ever had one and had to wash it nightly. The next day, Auntie Trina and seven girls went into Salisbury and she fitted me out with two extra ones.

While Uncle Ed worked at his tobacco, Auntie Trina kept a close watch on her chinchillas. I was very grateful I never saw any being killed and pelted.

I never really fitted in with any one of the children. I was fifteen, yet so much younger than Doreen who was my age and even younger than Moira who was a year younger than me and Sheila, who was older by a year. I fitted in better with the twins who were seven and Kathy who was eleven. I enjoyed being on the farm with all the other children. One night, I was crying and Uncle Ed found me and asked me had any of the other kids been mean to me. That was not the problem. I missed my mother and own sisters and brothers. I told him about my family and why I was in the Home. He said he would caress me if I allowed him. Not understanding what the word meant but that little inner voice once again told me it was not something I should allow him to do. Despite this, we did become very close.

While staying there, we all went to Beira three times. We had to have three chalets to accommodate us all. We all took great delight in all trying to pass off as one big family. Sometimes we thought we had got away with it. On our way back to the farm from our last Beira holiday Sheila and Moira who were in Auntie Trina's car were dropped off at the Home. Uncle Ed didn't like Sheila. She caught him kissing me. I felt terrible because when we all arrived at the farm Sheila and Moira weren't there. I knew nothing of the plan to take them both to the Home before the end of the holiday. Sheila also told Mrs. Tilbrook which I also found out much later that the reason why they were dropped off was because she had told his wife he was kissing me. When the holidays were over and I was taken back to the Home, Mrs. Tilbrook spoke to Auntie Trina in private and when they had left, Mrs. Tilbrook asked me to see her she said that Sheila and Moria were no longer to go to the Blanks but they were happy to still have me. I asked what they had done wrong. Mrs. Tilbrook said nothing they were just not going back. I had realised Shelia had seen Uncle Ed kissing me and felt I had betrayed them both. I didn't think that was very fair and wouldn't go out with the Blanks again. I was so confused, what was it about me that attracted these men to me, Why me?

Christmas 1970, I spent with Mr. and Mrs. Bould. These mishaps happen sometimes. Social Welfare had not done their homework properly. Mrs. Bould was a very heavy drinker and Mr. Bould was not in fact Mr. Bould at all. The man of the house was Mrs. Bould's boss. He had written her the letter of reference that was required by Social Welfare. Lynda, Mrs. Bould's daughter was my age, and I got on very well and kept in touch for a number of years. I was able to drive but had no licence. Lynda was still learning. More often than not, we would get a phone call from the publican at the social club to come and pick up Mrs. Bould as she was drunk and disorderly. When we were not playing taxi, we had a fantastic time. A ritual I still maintain today is to sit on a hill and watch the sun rise every New Year. Mrs. Tilbrook was very sorry about sending me out to a new home for six weeks without really knowing the family. She explained it was one of her more difficult tasks. It was very difficult to find suitable homes for the older girls. Some people had very young children and used us kids as their babysitters while other people were too old and had no company for us. She felt Mrs. Bould was suitable because she had a family and, best of all, a daughter my age. She asked me to forgive her. Gosh, fancy Mrs. Tilbrook asking me to forgive her! I was quite embarrassed and said it was alright, but she insisted that I forgave her. I didn't really see that forgiveness was in order, it was not her mistake but I said, "I forgive you."

The next holiday was the Easter weekend. Mrs. Tilbrook had found me another foster family. She told me a little bit about them, mainly that they were Swiss. In my mind, I had this dream building up, "Swiss Family Robinson" mixed in with a Swiss finishing school for young ladies. What a fantastic combination. They owned their own business, a motor car spray painting and panel beating shop. Mrs. Luginbuhl would be picking me up.

As we drove out of the circular driveway in the 220 petrol Mercedes Benz, I noticed Mrs. Luginbuhl's hands. They had never seen a finishing school, just very hard work. As I sat in silence, I took note of my driver. She was very confident, sat straight backed, and looked strong. Her eyes were kind and her hair thin and slightly grey. How old was she? She had had a hard life so perhaps she was younger than she looked. Not being able to work it out, I thought no more about it.

We arrived at Central Spray Painters to be greeted by two massive Alsatians. They bounded up to us, one jumping over the four foot counter and landing at our feet, while the other came broad siding through an open door. Both dogs leaped high in the air. One dog's claws caught my arm. Mrs. Luginbuhl shouted something in a language I had never heard. I was terrified. The dogs looked kind enough but just to stay on the safe side, I thought I would stick close to their mistress, that way I might survive the day. The two dogs were a team, Mischief, the bitch looked part wild, black-grey in colour with a sullen look on her face. Leo, although he was said to be the more vicious of the two, I took quickly to him. He was beautiful, a gold tan Alsatian, as big as a lion. Their job was to guard the workshop. The business had claimed numerous times off their insurance, it was suggested that they had the premises policed at night. This proved fruitless, as in many cases the man employed to do the job had many friends in the scrap metal business. It was then suggested that Mr. Luginbuhl kept two dogs there at all times.

Trudy, Mr. Luginbuhl's sister, had been collected by the driver and was waiting at the office for us. Trudy was older than Mrs. Luginbuhl, she was quite grey, her curly hair thicker than Mrs. Luginbuhl's hair, she was also of a slimmer build. She always smoked a cigarette protruding out of a silver black cigarette holder. She was very quietly spoken. In fact, I have never heard her ever raise her voice or get over anxious in any situation. Trudy was introduced to me as Trudy and I never enquired what her other name was for a number of years. Trudy and I got along very well. She helped to bridge some gaps between Mrs. Luginbuhl and me, those first few weeks. Her English was far superior and also she had had children of her own and knew more about our needs. Trudy and her late husband owned and managed the Hartley Hotel in Hartley. They were so highly thought of that when they sold it to the Meikles Group of Hotels and built a large house in the expanding town of Hartley, the people of Hartley named one of the streets Llanigan Drive.

Trudy said that we were going to Mana Pools for Easter and that Gus was already there. Seeing the questioning look on my face she explained who Gus was. Mr. Luginbuhl played football in Switzerland and because his name was such a mouthful to say, his friends called him Gus. It was taken out of his middle name Gustav. Mrs. Luginbuhl had adopted the name of Mrs. Gus. Trudy always said it was easier to say as well as spell. I opted for the easier of the two. Today my own two sons only know them as Gus and Mrs. Gus.

After feeding the dogs the biggest meal I have ever seen two dogs eat and leaving two large bowls of water, we locked the place up and made our way to Mana Pools. Mrs. Gus drove very fast, and in no time at all, we were out of Salisbury and on our way through the Great Dyke.

The Great Dyke is a chain of granite hills which stretches through the middle of Rhodesia from Sipilelo in the north to Belingwe in the south. These hills are said to be very rich in minerals, copper, gold, and chrome are mined from them. Many other minerals exist there too but they are either too deep into the rock or in too small a quantity. Uranium is one such metal.

Leaving the Great Dyke behind, the next town we passed through Banket then Sinoia and Karoi. We stopped at Makuti to fill the car with petrol and then went on to Chirundu and finally we arrived at Mana Pools in the late afternoon. We found the campsite but Gus was out on the boat, fishing. The servants that Gus had taken up with him helped us to unload the car. Mrs. Gus, Trudy, and I had something to drink and made up the beds before the men came back. I found that there were a number of different Swiss families there, including Mrs. Gus's sister and her children, Mrs. Thutu, Heidi and her married brother with his wife and two small children. What confusion! Gus is a German Swiss, Mrs. Gus is French Swiss and so is her family then somewhere in the middle of all this were the different village dialects and little me! How I longed to be back at the Home. I thought, "First, the dogs nearly eat me for lunch and now I am to be sent to Coventry. Everyone is talking so fast in their own language and they are quite oblivious to me." I managed to sit the night out, Trudy reminding them every now and then to talk English. Then there would be a deadly hush as they thought of something to say. Trudy found it easier most of the time just to tell me what the different topics were about.

In the morning, I was woken up by the strong sunlight streaming into our tents. The day was bright and the sun quite warm, small droplets of water still lay on the shaded spider's webs. The camp had not quite woken and everything was very quiet. Mrs. Gus was already up and so too was Trudy but Heidi and Gus were still asleep. I got dressed and went to the toilets to have a wash. Mrs. Gus was at the main tent preparing breakfast. By the time, I had finishing washing it was as if a bell had been rung, the whole camp was alive. In the light of the new day, however the confusion of the previous night was gone. People were talking more slowly and everyone asked me how I had slept. Mrs. Gus said that at one time she had thought of throwing Gus out of the tent because of his snoring. She had then realized it was not Gus but someone outside. They all told her it was a lion. I had slept very well without waking.

After breakfast, we all went out on the boat except for Heidi's brother's wife and the small children. Mrs. Gus and Trudy also stayed behind.

On our trip up the river, we noticed some people skiing and thought it would be fun but we had no skis, though we did have a large Kaylite board (Kaylite——polystyrene). We thought we would make use of it. Tying a rope to the boat, we lay on the board holding the other end of the rope we would then wave Gus on. Heidi went first. Then she persuaded me to go. It was frightening but fun. I panicked, my arms got very tired. What could I do? I shouted and shouted but they just went faster and faster. It took me sometime to realise that all I had to do was let go and tread water till they came back and picked me up. We spent all morning up and down the river, coming in for lunch. Gus and some of the other men disappeared in the boat with all their fishing tackle. Heidi and I sat on the riverbank and fished and talked till we heard the boat coming back. The language problem of the day before didn't seem to exist. We had fewer people at our dinner table that night and ate some freshly cooked bream with our boiled potatoes made into rösti (the closest I can come to this dish in English is similar to a hash brown).

Saturday was very quiet. The men had all gone fishing early in the morning. We all sat around the camp. Trudy and Mrs. Gus had their knitting, Heidi had a book, and I walked within sight of the camp returning every now and then with my finds of birds' nests, driftwood and other objects. Mrs. Gus and Trudy's knitting intrigued me. They had very big round knitting needles and it reminded me more of crocheting than knitting. Their work seemed to grow very fast. It was fascinating to see the sleeves grafted on to the rest of the garment. Unlike my knitting, they ended up with a completely finished item with no stitching up to do at all.

Gus and the other men came in with the boat, just as the sun was setting. Gus was in some pain, he had trodden on a barbel which lay in the boat. One of its dorsal fin spines had gone into his foot.

We had a quiet dinner. Mrs. Gus and Trudy talked to Gus about our day. Gus, affectionately, put his hand on my head and ruffled my hair. "She is alright, this one," he said. "Very frightened of people but we will get her on Choby, that will give her some confidence." Heidi worked for Mrs. Gus in the office at Central Spray Painters and also lived with them at Edelweiss Farm. The farm was near Ruwa, just outside Salisbury. Thinking back to that first meeting and Gus's confidence in me reminds me of Ouma Benadie. She once gave my mother some very pretty curtains and as she passed them over she said, "I am sorry you have such a heavy cross to carry but one day you will find your Prince Charming, just like Cinderella on these curtains." I found my Prince Charming in these two people. I realised this now.

Mrs. Gus took me home after lunch on Easter Sunday. The very best Easter Sunday I have ever had. Easter Sunday was more special than even Christmas. Mrs. Gus boiled three dozen eggs and Saturday evening, when we had all gone to bed, she sat and painted them all. Early Sunday morning she hid them all over the camp. To this day, I don't know what told me to stay in the tent that little longer than the other mornings. I woke up, got dressed, and walked to the flap of the tent. Mrs. Gus was in her dressing gown with a basket in one hand, it looked as if she was hiding something. I thought to myself, I don't think I am meant to see that but then again, I am really bursting to go to the loo. I did however just go and sit on my bed till I heard Mrs. Gus coming back to the tent.

After breakfast, Trudy explained that we had to hunt for our Easter eggs. Then I put it together, the three dozen eggs, Mrs. Gus, and the basket. I felt so good I had not spoilt her surprise. This should be easy, white eggs in the bush, I thought. So I went to the place that I had seen Mrs. Gus at that morning but found a real surprise. The eggs were painted, browns, greens, yellows, some even spotted. The search went on for some hours. My biggest thrill was my very own basket. It contained bunny rabbit eggs, a decorated egg with sugar flowers and maiden hair fern, marshmallow eggs and my name painted on one of the eggs. Easter remains a very special time for me, ever since that Easter of 1969.

After my Easter weekend with Mrs. Gus, the Home was more like boarding school and each holiday that followed I went home to Edelweiss, to my new foster parents. During the week, I went into the office with them. At first, I was so frightened I spent most of the day reading magazines in a room Mrs. Gus had set aside for me. It took me a long time to find the courage to pick up the telephone and answer it take the different messages and pass them on. Over the weekends, Mrs. Gus and I spent many hours doing one thing or another on the farm. Gus generally tried to stay out of the way, sometimes fishing or at the small bore rifle shooting.

One of my jobs, which I did enjoy, was driving the Land Rover with two, forty-four gallon drums of water in the back of it. The Land Rover had lost its original number plates and its disc was sixteen years old. The Land Rover never left the farm so we never bothered to tax or insure it. Even through the rainy season, the garden had to be watered at least once a week. Most flower gardens needed watering every day. The fruit trees had to be watered as long as the water was available. Sometimes the dam would get so low that we could not pump it up to the house. The well that Gus made was then put to full use. I would water the fruit trees from the water in the two drums on the Land Rover. It was not advisable to syphon it out this water wasn't clean. Plunging a two gallon bucket in to the water and watering the trees guaranteed every tree received two gallons once a week.

I think, really, I enjoyed driving the Land Rover more than the actual task. I had learnt to drive properly on the Blank's farm but had really been driving since I was twelve. Living on the farm, driving is a very necessary part of living. To be able to sit on a cushion and reach the pedals and not drive, one is about as useful as a cow that could not be milked. I stayed mainly on the farm roads, though people without a licence including myself, have driven into the city centre, when it has been essential. Betty, I believe, saved Oupa Theron's life making just such a journey. In 1969, she brought him in to Salisbury, travelling from Macheke. Arriving at the hospital, he was taken into emergency theatre. He had a brain tumour. I drove without a licence until I was nineteen.

The Rhodesian Traffic Law was slightly different to British law and Australian Law. Anyone may have a licence once they turn sixteen.

No matter what cc motorcycle one rides, even for a moped, one needs a motorcycle licence.

The Gus's belonged to the Swiss Club. The first of August being the Swiss National Day would call for a huge party. It always took place over the first weekend in August. Generally these parties were held at the farm. Once, just before the Swiss Consulate was recalled to Switzerland it was held at his house. The different Swiss traditions were followed, together with a good Rhodesian braai. Just as in the Italian and Portuguese Clubs it was not strange to find English speaking Rhodesians at these functions. Our party started off with the small bore rifle shooting during the day. The range, although it was on our farm, belonged to the First Battalion Rifle Club. Lunch was served usually by Mrs. Gus and the other wives at midday from the small but efficient kitchen on the range. The whole area became a massive picnic ground. Everyone forgot the intense competition of the morning's shoot and bought beers for the best and even worst shot.

The day's shooting closed, with the different prizes being given. A party at the house was to be the next event. The bustle inside the house was not apparent as they drove up the drive. The two flagpoles, which for most of the year stood stark and white, had their flags flying proudly. The Swiss White Cross on its red background was in striking contrast to the alternating green, white, and green vertical stripes of the Rhodesian Flag, with its coat of arms displayed on the white centre stripe. The sun set taking with it its light. Twilight lasted for such a short time, no one admired it. Many coloured lights, hidden high in the trees round the house, changed the features of the old thatched farmhouse. The outside ten pin bowling alley was always an attraction. The weather was kind most National days for which we were thankful. The bowling alley had no roof on it. A piccaninny sat on the low wall and picked up the skittles, placing them carefully on the white round spots marking their places, after each throw.

During the evening the Swiss Consulate would give a speech in German, French, and English, and then a tape was played which had been sent from Switzerland, closing off with the Swiss National Anthem. The whole day's entertainment ended with most women finding a bed in one of the five bedrooms for the children, while the men played cards well into the early hours of the morning. Once, a card game was still in action while Mrs. Gus and I had Sunday breakfast.

Most of the salads and food for these parties always came from Mr. Sieler. He owned a bakery in Msasa, one of the industrial sites of Salisbury. One dish which always appeared and was by far the tastiest was the ham. (Mrs. Gus had built her own smokehouse, the design for which came from a smokehouse she had in Switzerland.)

Gus usually killed one of the farm pigs. Once and only once did Gus ask me to stir the pig's blood. The pig hung from the rafters with its throat slashed. The very thought, reminds me of *Lord of the Flies*. The blood gushed out at first, filling the large barrel quickly, a deep rich red thick, warm, blood smelling liquid. "Stir it quickly," shouted Gus, "don't let it get thick," Stirring the blood with a long thick paddle like plank, the blood began slowly to change. Thick pink frothy bubbles started to stick to the sides of the barrel. Then, slowly, the whole barrel was covered with thick pink bubbles, fighting for space, one popping as a newer, more solid bubble forced its way to the top. As it popped, small particles of blood spotted me and any other nearby admirers. My arms became tired, I was angry and repulsed by my task. Mrs. Gus thought I did a wonderful job but I later confessed to Gus that I would never do it again. The blood had to be stirred till it was room temperature, ensuring that it coagulated evenly. The blood was later used for bloed wurst (black pudding). The pig was then scraped while it was still warm to remove all the hair from the part we know as the rind. Large metal spoons were used. They had been used for so many pigs, they almost did the job without a guide. One person's sole job was to pour the boiling water over sections on the pig while two others scraped fast and hard, removing all the long coarse, thick white hairs. When the pig was very clean it was washed with soap and water, then taken out of that room on to a chopping block. Its head was cut off and it was gutted. Mrs. Gus and I then sectioned the pig. At first, I was not allowed to cut any part but was a good holder. Later I got the job of cutting the trotters off. Whole thighs were left intact, they would be the hams. The skin covering the rib cage was used for smoked bacon. The liver was made into liverwurst (liver sausage); that I did enjoy eating but will never eat black pudding. The thought of it takes me back to stirring that barrel of blood. The different pieces that were to be smoked were cured in large barrels of brine. They seemed to be there for ages, they were taken out to the smokehouse and smoked for a number of weeks. Mrs. Gus always looked after the smoking personally, adding sawdust daily to the pile already smouldering. She always bought her sawdust from a particular sawmill, maintaining the different trees gave the meat a certain flavour. The best ham was selected and Mr. Sieler cooked it in his oven. The outer, brown, toughened, smoked skin was never removed it added to the flavour. A good thick layer of bread dough was placed over the whole thigh and cooked for many hours. It was best, eaten hot. The bread closest to the ham was moist and slightly doughy, like dumplings in a stew soaking up the meat juices. Closer to the crust it was more bread like. Smoked ham flavoured bread is delicious!

Mrs. Gus was an extra ordinary person. She had the physical stamina that would put most men to shame. Rising at five, she would see to it that the few cows were milked. We only had a few. They gave us about three to four gallons of milk a day. She would then separate most of the milk saving the cream for butter. This was made in a large glass jar which had a handle attached to its lid and butterfly type wooden beaters which churned the cream round. The buttermilk and milk which we didn't use went to the pigs, dogs, and 'eleventeen' cats. She sometimes sold a pint or two to some of the Africans on the farm but said that it cost her more, substituting those few pints with pig feed it was not worth the trouble.

During the week, she transformed herself into an unpaid office lady, running her side of the office which included collecting and delivering different cars and all the clerical side of the business. Mrs. Gus dealt with the accountant, and later on, I found out it was her own money which financed the business. It was while on one of these errands just shortly after I began spending my holidays with them, that Mrs. Gus and I were involved in a slight mishap with another car. We had stopped at the robots (traffic lights) when another car hit us from behind. The second driver got a little bad tempered with Mrs. Gus so she had someone call the police. After giving the usual verbal descriptions, a statement was taken. It was then that I learnt Mrs. Gus's age—fifty-nine years.

I was horrified. She worked so hard, never showing any signs of ever giving up. The thought of her age struck in my mind and my thoughts flashed back to the time she separated Buster, Trudy's bulldog, and Tiny one of her more vicious Alsatians. She twisted Buster's tail as she watched and waited. Buster released his hold on Tiny. Mrs. Gus still holding on to his tail grabbed him by the scruff of the neck as she picked up this solid British bulldog known for never letting go and simultaneously kicked Tiny. Trudy arrived with Buster's chain and took charge of him. Tiny not content still wanted to continue the fight was pushed into the nearest car and the door closed. My thoughts still fixed firmly on her stamina. I thought of the time she broke her wrist while building the horse stable but because she was adamant and wanted them done for a certain date she strapped her hand up and completed the job. Later that evening, she drove herself to 'out patients' and had it set. She did not only do all the physical tasks round the farm but also did the sewing, knitting, and did the most beautiful embroidery. She was one in a million.

It would be unfair not to mention Gus, for he too was a character. Gus would work, but only at what was important to him. He was very quiet, and it took me a long time to get to know him. He lived by many of his own philosophies. Gus always maintained there was no God. God is your conscience. If you can honestly say you have acted within your conscience and you can sleep at night, you are a good person, beyond reproach from your fellow men. This has compounded my own belief. People say God will punish you for xyz. I do believe he does not punish anyone there is no need. He gave us a conscience, we punish ourselves. The other very sound bit of advice which he gave me was there isn't such a thing as love. It's respect however love and respect go hand in hand. In a partnership, especially marriage, when one person had no respect for the other then it's time to throw the towel in. His philandering he put down to the fact that no one could maintain a diet of purely cabbage.

Gus respected Madeleine and she too must have respected certain things about him perhaps the philosophical way in which he looked at life, enabled her to overlook the weaker points.

Gus was the main animal lover. Mrs. Gus would see to their needs, but it was Gus who had an affinity with them. Gus had a donkey once. The animal must have thought it was a dog and as the dogs had the run of the house so did the donkey. If ever we left a door open, the animal would look for Gus inside. Things went flying as he strutted through the house. At breakfast time, if we ever forgot to give him his toast and marmalade, he almost broke the door down. It was a shame, but when we got the horses, he went a bit peculiar. At first we thought he had just taken an offence to the horses, when he insisted on sleeping with the cows but then he became very nasty. Someone said we ought to have him castrated. This was done but he became even more bad tempered. Eventually, we had to have him put to sleep. Mrs. Gus had said that one day he would kill someone. Gus then got a goat. I was told he was eating everything, fresh flowers as well as plastic ones. Mrs. Gus has had to take down her best velvet curtains. Gus and I went for long walks in the bush with him so that he could eat food which was natural to him as he was constantly getting kidney stones and was a regular visitor to the vet.

Our first horse was Choby, the most lovable cart horse. He was always so gentle, and almost anyone could ride him from the very young to good experienced riders. Sheila was the second addition. At times she was a cantankerous hag and only a good rider was suitable for her. Then we acquired Eric and Capie Express. They were two racehorses. Capie Express was the gentler of the two. He had broken his leg and rather than see them shot, Mrs. Gus said she would have them. They were both going to be shot because Eric refused to run without Capie Express. Both horses were geldings but very different in temperament. When we first got them, very few people could ride Eric. He was seventeen hands and had the strength of an ox. We had him for a number of years before I was able to ride him or even wanted to. The second time I went out on him, he bolted home. Jumping all the farm gates, he made straight for his stable. Then at the last second, almost before he stopped dead, he broadsides I was still holding on for dear life. He had had enough. He gave an almighty buck and I went flying through the air. Realising the wall and I were about to become close acquaintances, I turned my body in mid air and came crushing down, banging my left arm on the stable wall. Mrs Gus and I had had a mother and daughter tiff that morning one of the reasons I was out riding by myself. Mrs. Gus thought I had deliberately gone against something she had told one of the other children. They wanted to shorten one of their dresses and had come to ask me to help them. They had previously asked and were told they were not allowed to do it. Unwittingly, I was caught in the middle. Mrs. Gus was deeply disappointed by my actions and yet she was the first person to come to my aid. This was a new concept to me. I dislocated my elbow. Never again did I ride Eric. I stuck to my cantankerous mare. At least I could read her eye and knew when I was in for a rough ride, unlike Eric. That too was my last tiff with Mrs. Gus.

While living on the farm, Choby showed signs of getting very old. No one was allowed to ride him, not even the smallest child. Mrs. Gus noticed that he was slightly lame and so when the other horses were let out, Choby was kept in. Later, during the day, Mrs. Gus was phoned from the farm. Choby was unable to stand. I took the rest of the day off work and went out with the vet. Choby lay on the ground just outside his stable. The very young assistant vet said Choby was just too old and it was really the kindest thing to do. He could leave him though he felt sure he would die during the night. Sitting on the ground with Choby's head in my lap, I talked to him while the vet put him to sleep. Choby looked at me with his watery eyes then looked away and closed his eyelids. The silence was broken by Sheila rattling the wooden pole at the gate with her head. I said to the vet, "I wonder if she has come because she knows her friend has died?" He said, "She more than likely thought she would get an extra handful of oats, so let's not disappoint her." With that, we both took her a handful of horse cubes. Choby was buried at the far side of the shooting range.

It was while I was working that Capie Express met with an accident. Mrs. Gus had employed an African to be their stable boy. He soon noticed Capie's love of jumping, something we never encouraged because of his once broken leg. Mrs. Gus came home one Friday to find Capie in a lot of pain; he had broken his leg jumping over some fences, while the African was riding him. Capie had to be put down. Shortly after Capie's accident, Eric got very bad colic and though Mrs. Gus spent a whole night with him in his stable, he died the following morning. Sheila was very lonely and often went over to the next door farm, returning in the evening, until one night she never came home. Mrs. Gus went to our neighbours the next day. They agreed to keep her. I had left home by now, and Mrs Gus didn't have the time to spend with her.

Trudy came to stay once she had sold her large house near the Blue Gardenia which was a drive-in restaurant in Mabelreign. Our biggest problem was Buster. He was not liked by all the other dogs, including the bitches. They all went for him as soon as he showed his face. Tiny was the worst. We would have to lock our dogs up while Buster had his afternoons as Trudy used to say. Eventually Rex accepted him but we always had to watch Tiny. Rex had a terrible habit of chasing the cows, in fact any livestock. He never, ever, killed anything and always knew when to leave. One afternoon the boar got out and, of course, Rex was there to greet him but so was Buster. Only Buster did not know the rules of the game. Mrs. Gus said that it was because the likeness was too much for him to bear. He had to show his superiority. The bull dog not having the speed that most dogs would have could not get out of the way quick enough. The boar gored him badly. I didn't know this till we took him to the vet, a bull dog's flesh cannot be stitched. Its flesh is too soft and just tears as the sutures pull the flesh together. Buster was very badly hurt and even after a blood transfusion, he died that night. The boar weighed over nine hundred pounds. We had been given him to service our sows but he was so heavy they just buckled under his weight so the idea was that when the freezer had sufficient place in it, he would be slaughtered. He did make some good hams and liverwurst. Poor Buster, he didn't really stand a chance. The moral of the story is "pick on someone your own size."

Mrs. Gus went through a number of servants, as do many other Rhodesians. One evening, after returning from work, there was a well dressed African waiting to see her. Tembo wanted a job. He had good references and could start the next day but would need time off that weekend to collect his wife and belongings. Tembo, unbeknown to Mrs. Gus, was a CID African. He had been told to get a job in our area and to find the dagga (marijuana) growers. Which he did. Several months later, one Sunday, we were woken by dogs barking and Land Rovers driving up the driveway. Tembo had found nearly twenty acres, most of it on our farm. Though our plot had ninety acres most of it was granite rock. We never did a lot with the land it was more a place to stay as would be a house in the suburb. All our Africans were taken away and so were the Africans from the next door farm. From the time that Tembo had found it and then reported his find, someone had harvested quite a lot. The rest was burnt by the police. The African who said it was his was sent to jail. He worked on the next farm. Tembo was so pleased with himself. He asked us to come and see him get his mendol (medal). Mrs. Gus wouldn't go but Keith, my boyfriend, did. Being in the forces, even if it was the Territorial Force, he appreciated the importance of Tembo's mendol. Mrs. Gus felt betrayed and was annoyed. To show her displeasure, she refused to go. It was expected that I would follow her example and never went either.

Nineteen seventy was my last year at school, my O level year. I had worked hard and seemed to have to work harder than most of the other children who appeared to manage to stay at the top end of the class results. Fort Vic was a small school and while I had managed to be in the top 10 in my stream I was just not making the grade anymore. Now that I am older and know something about the many different aspects of learning, I can tie my poor reading in with the many difficulties which I encountered at school.

During my second year at Roosevelt School, Mrs. Mackenzie, our English teacher, picked up my poor reading. In the two years of being at Roosevelt School, I only ever read out aloud once. With as much tact as an over confident bully, she called me out of the line, just before entering her class. "Go down to Mrs. Beeson's class, take all your books, you are to do some reading for her." A long awkward silence followed as she waited for me to leave. I knew she meant me but I just stood my ground. Mrs. Beeson taught the 'special class.' The class was made up of a few children but all of different ages. While most of us felt certain obligations to these children, none, really wanted to be seen dead in their classroom. The special class was mainly for children who had a very low IQ. Some had a mental handicap though not that severe as to warrant going to any special schools like Saint Giles. "Myrna, do as you are told!" she said. "I am not going to Mrs. Beeson," I heard myself saying defiantly. "I have told you to do something, either go to Mrs. Beeson or see Miss Robertson in her office!" Now I have done it, I thought. Well, Mrs. Beeson wasn't that bad, not quite as bad as Miss Robertson, the head mistress.

I walked slowly away, hoping I would fall down and break a leg. I could still feel all thirty-two pairs of eyes on me. The corridors were empty except for Five B. Then, slowly and quietly, little whispers started. They were interrupted, "That's enough. In you go," boomed Mrs. Mackenzie's voice. As the classroom door closed, I looked back along the empty corridor and quickened my pace. If I walked as though I had a purpose, people were less likely to know I was going to Mrs. Beeson's class.

Mrs. Beeson was kind and quietly spoken. She asked me to wait in one of her spare classrooms. Once she had settled her class she came in and closed the door. I was then asked to read a sheet of words, getting more complicated and smaller in print, the further down the page they went. Mrs. Beeson then explained that I had a reading age of nine, though I was almost seventeen, and in theory, it should be higher by several years than one's chronological age. I didn't really understand but was horrified, thinking I was only able to read what a nine-year-old child read. I told Mrs. Beeson that I had had reading tests like the one she had asked me to read but was always told I was average. Mrs. Beeson said she didn't know how they had arrived at that conclusion. To begin with, I returned daily after school. I told Mrs. Tilbrook it was for extra work. Then as I got more used to the idea of going to Mrs. Beeson's class I agreed to go during my free periods at school. Other than reading and working from a Reading Laboratory, not a lot was done. Mrs. Beeson, at one point, said that I had reached as high a standard as I could go with her. Though I needed a lot more, the school just did not cater for pupils in an O level stream with my problem. Her children only went up to school leaver exams, which consisted of an English and Arithmetic exam, most doing it at sixteen while others took until they were seventeen to pass it. She also said that I really had far more work than I could cope with. I changed schools in the middle of my O level syllabus which meant a lot of catching up.

In November 1970, 17 years old, I wrote my eight O level subjects. (This is equivalent to eight year twelve subjects.) At Fort Victoria High, I dropped history and took bookkeeping but at Roosevelt I had to take history. Bookkeeping was not an option for children in a B stream. History was a subject that I had a constant struggle with and as I had to catch up two years work, I decided right from the outset that it was one lesson in which I could do other work. My English Literature was another subject which called upon my skills. I had been a genius, up till Mrs. Mackenzie came on the scene, working out how not to get picked to read out aloud in class. Reading out aloud was a fate worse than death for me. I watched and saw how each teacher worked the classroom then worked that to my advantage. I found if one sat quietly and never drew attention one got passed over more often than not. I paid others to read my books to me. More often than not it was a Bata System. I would do things like sewing while they read my set books. Geography was another subject which needed a lot of extra work. At Fort Victoria, we started with the African Continent while Roosevelt had started on Europe. Finding the subject difficult, it was even more difficult to motivate myself to stick with it. So as time went on, I persisted with the subjects which I found I could understand and have an affinity with, namely biology, Afrikaans, and Needlework. Though Afrikaans was a second language to me, I got all three subjects on my O level certificate. I left school at the end of 1970, still hoping I would get my English O level. I went nursing but after rewriting English in June 1971 and failing it again, I went out into the wide world. I lived with Mrs. Gus and started working and training as a bookkeeper. Deep down, I still wanted to pursue my nursing dream. I went to night school and resat my English for a third time in November 1971 but once again failed. That was the end of my nursing dream. Mrs. Klette tried to talk me into sticking with my nursing career. She was on the Home Committee. Once I had left school, Mr. and Mrs. Klette and I built up a lasting friendship. It was then that Mr. Klette said he wished he had known about my reading, he would have been able to help. I am not sure why to this day the school did not inform the Home of my reading problems. Mr. Klette said being the secretary to the Minister of Education and his wife being on the board of directors at the Home, his position would have given him a lot of power.

My poor reading skills have dogged me all my life. I felt it so very important to read to my children. I only did this task when they were very small and I could fake what I was reading. Before they were able to read themselves, I would choose a book with only pictures and would make up the story from the pictures. I stopped reading to them when Mark started correcting me. This was now time for Keith to take on the task.

'Mapandas'

I met Keith while I was nursing, in February 1971. Apart from going to Mrs. Gus on my days and weekends off, it was the first time I went out with the other nurses. There were three of us and Dot Smyth agreed to pick us up. On the way to the Young Rhodesians Social Club our driver was telling us how and when the club began and the different things they all did, varying from a paper chase to bingo nights, dances, and braais. Alex Basant asked her what the talent was like. Dot replied that she had met her husband at one of the functions. Alex then turned to me and said, "Watch out, Myrna, tonight you will come home with a husband!" I was so embarrassed, being the quietest and extremely shy. I sunk low into the backseat and said nothing.

The dance started with a snowball. Dot and Bruce Smyth were the first couple. They split up, taking on two fresh wallflowers. Then Dot noticed Alex and me still sitting down. She brought her partner over, introduced him to Alex and I sighed with relief. Some time passed and Alex was standing in front of me with the same partner. Bending down she whispered, "He's more your age. Myrna, please dance with him." I thought how terrible Alex's manners were and remembered Trudy once telling me how very rude it was to refuse a man a dance, saying that it takes a tremendous amount of courage to walk from one end of the room to the other and ask a girl for a dance. The least we women could do was to have the courtesy to accept and with that I danced with Keith.

In December, Keith's entire family went to Vumba near Umtali. Mrs. Seagrave, after meeting my Social Welfare officer, was given permission to take me as well. We all stayed in a very big cottage in the Vumba Mountains. There were ten of us and on Christmas Day, John, Keith's older brother, and his wife and family arrived.

The Vumba, in my mind is the most beautiful part of Rhodesia. The rainfall is high, giving rise to some exceptional flora. It is one of the highest parts of Rhodesia. This accounts for its cooler climate. Most of the wild orchids grew there. The leopard orchid is the most popular. The flowers striking sun yellow petals spotted with brown splashes is a pretty contrast against the green foliage of the trees in which it is found. Many different wild species of gladioli are found in the Vumba. All these flowers and many English flowers are grown in the very large botanical gardens set in the Vumba Mountains, together with one of the oldest living plants, which can still be found growing in the wild, the Cycad. The Cycad is, perhaps, something like a palm tree but very much smaller, some being over three hundred and fifty million years old. All the vegetation was so different to what I had lived with whilst in the Lowveld. The plants no longer had hostile sharp thorns and spines but delicate soft leaves and flowers that lasted more than a day. The abundance of water gave the whole area a friendly, warm, welcoming look. Plants fought for light not water. The flame lily's tendrils twisted round a stronger plant showing its spectacular yellow red petals. The edges rippled and twisted like the flame from a gypsy's campfire. They almost looked as if they flickered and danced as they curled upwards away from the stigma and stamens. Such splendid beauty, we did well to name it our national flower.

As we looked over the pine trees at the bottom of the garden, towards the mountains, the morning mist was still lingering. The clouds were so low no one appreciated just how high the mountains really were. Some of the higher mountains would have their heads in the clouds all day. The Africans say Vumba means Mist. We Europeans adopted the nickname of Mountains of Mist, when we wished to speak of Vumba poetically. That's what the whole area looked like, not mountains of trees, rocks, and grass but Mountains of Mist.

One of the more popular hotels was Leopard Rock Hotel, so named because the very large rocky outcrop behind the hotel was the home of many leopards. Leopard Rock could be seen from our cottage. A worthwhile walk was from the cottage, past the pine trees, and through the forest of hydrangeas at the far end of our garden. The hydrangeas grew profusely. So intense was their forest that a number of freaks sprung up from the constant close pollination which occurred when the large bumblebee collected its nectar. Not only were there the sugar almond colours but deep mauves and scarlets, pale blues almost white, then the smallest freak, the all green hydrangea. The more conventional hydrangeas towered above us, some growing to five and six foot shrubs. Walking through the bush took anything from two hours to well into the afternoon depending on how fast we walked and how many stops we made. A welcome end to the walk was the ice cold drink at Leopard Rock Hotel. That's the best part, the bar's opening hours were from half past ten and closing when the last person left so we never had to coincide our walks with pub hours, if we wanted a drink at the end.

The hotel was set just under the large rocky outcrop. Its brick coloured walls were almost entirely covered in creeping ivy. The terraced garden was a mass of coloured sun umbrellas with the car park a short distance away. To the left of the hotel, shadowed by the towering leopard rock, was the most exquisite water garden with high spraying fountains, banana palms, and Japanese imperial carp. The deep blue and white slender bodied fish, gracefully swimming in and out of the many exotic water lilies, were fascinating to watch. Some of the older fish were going through their colour change. There was a mixture of colours, some red and white, others red, orange, and black. In Japan, some of these fish are auctioned for fantastic sums of money. Our journey home was, to the Africans, suicidal. We climbed Leopard Rock and walked a short distance back on to the road and the cottage was two miles further up the road. We never encountered any leopards. The locals were always very surprised to see us the next day. They always said we must have walked around the rock. They maintained that had the leopards not killed us then the spirits would, so we must have walked around and not over.

Keith and my holiday was shorter than the rest of the family. Neither of us had been able to take extra leave, and Keith being in the Territorial Army also had to go on a weekend parade. I thought they were a complete waste of time. Fancy having to run from the Drill Hall through town to the Rhodesian Light Infantry headquarters some five miles, then go over an obstacle course which included a twelve foot wall. They had to climb up and jump down. Keith chipped a bone in his heel doing just that and was off work and the army for six weeks. During this time, Keith and I saw a lot of each other. We set our wedding date for June 6, 1972.

Getting married posed more problems than I ever thought possible. I had too many loyalties. The right and proper thing to do would be to have Adam give me away. He had, after all, been my father, however bad a father he was, since I was five years old. My own father had dropped out of my life just as dramatically as he had announced himself that evening at Fort Victoria. Then there was Gus. Both Gus and Mrs. Gus had picked me up turned me round and shown me what parents should be like. They had begun to look at me as one of the family. I told Mrs Gus what I wished to do. My wish was that Gus would give me away. I also told her my fears. This led me to my ultimate choice, the idea stolen from one of the other Home girls. One of the committee members would have to do the honour. Now I had to find my favourite. Mr. Klettle came up tops.

With the tremendous help of Keith's family, Trudy, Mrs. Gus, and Keith, the build up to our wedding was taking shape. Trudy helped me make my dress. Mrs. Seagrave showed me how to ice my cake after Nanna, Keith's gran, baked it, and Mrs. Gus paid for our reception. Some weeks before the set date, strange things began to happen at work. Mrs. Mackie, my senior, would get a phone call. After a short and abrupt conversation, I was given a very trivial task to do. At times, I thought of rebelling. However, I always did the tasks, and they always included leaving the office. One Saturday, Keith said his sister needed some help with one of the kid's parties, could I help? Never giving it too much thought, I agreed and arrived at Pat's house to find a sitting room full of women. There were the girls from work, matrons from the Home, Mrs. Klettle, Mrs. Tilbrook, and Mrs. Gus to name but a few. Keith and Mrs. Mackie had, while I was set trivial tasks, arranged my kitchen tea. Traditionally, this would have been the bridesmaid's pleasure but as our wedding was to be on such a small scale, we were not having many frills and fancies.

The gifts that really stuck in my mind were a book *Cookery in Colour* by Marguerite Patten given to me by Mrs. Tilbrock. This book is still a big part of my collection of cookery books and very well used. The other was a doll made up from all kitchen utensils/items which Mrs. Gus made. The body was a round grater and inside that was an egg whisk with the old fashioned handle on top and on the side was a small handle that you used to turn the beaters. A wooden spoon was attached with a yellow duster which was made to look like her scarf. She had tea towels folded into a typical Swiss ladies bonnet and her skirt was made up of tea towels which covered her well placed yellow plastic pot scorers. She had an apron on which was folded in such a way as to have pockets. Inside them were a few clothes pegs. My doll sat in my kitchen until she became so dusty she no longer did justice to Mrs. Gus's hard work. I washed her but could never manage to reconstruct her.

Keith has always been the more considerate partner, making up many different anniversaries like our second week anniversary or six month anniversary. He tried always to make it more special than the last, sometimes ending a beautiful meal with one of his special poems:

> "20:8:1971
> Myrna,
> With Rose petals,
> They make Wine,
> and tonight with my cookie,
> I did dine.
> Keith."

At the end of the evening, the waiter collected the menu as he cleared our table and poured our coffee. The manager returned handing me the menu saying, "I presume this is yours." Then he turned to Keith and said, "And you, sir, will have an added service charge on your bill, for defacing our menu!" Keith looked very shocked, and I sat smiling at the manager as he turned away and winked at me. From that night, I would always make sure and ask for a menu as a souvenir.

Nineteen seventy-two, Tuesday, June 6, had arrived. The day was bright with clear skies. The mid-winter's day had a cool brisk wind. Everything seemed to be going well. Mr. and Mrs. Klettle drove me to the church. The minister greeted us outside and I asked him if my parents had arrived. Father Fenick, not knowing them, said he didn't know. I described my mother, stepfather, brother, and sisters to him. Returning a short while later, he said they were not in the church. After waiting for what seemed like eternity, Father Fenick said it didn't seem fair to make my whole day late because of late arrivals. With that, Mrs. Klettle went inside. Mr. Klettle, the minister, and I walked in. As soon as I joined Keith, I whispered, "Keith, my mum's not here." Keith turned round to look at the rather empty church. "I am sorry," he said, squeezing my hand. I had no more strength left in me to fight the tears back and cried right through the entire service. Mrs. Klettle managed to repair my makeup in the very few seconds before we signed the register. The irony of it all was I had wanted my wedding to be mid-week and early morning so that I would have no scenes brought about by a stepfather who couldn't hold his liquor and a father who also drank excessively. Neither of them arrived, and it was I who made the scene, emerging red eyed and complaining of a headache. Father Fenick, admitted much later that he was very unsure as to whether I had agreed to the marriage. He had never seen a girl cry so much. No excuse or reason for any of them not turning up on the day was ever given.

The rest of the day went off very well. Keith and I left the reception with Brandy, my six week puppy. Keith had rented a beautiful cottage in Inyanga. Inyanga is not as far north as Vumba and not so wooded. We had a fantastic week of cascading waterfalls, and hill walks. Keith sensing my day was not as happy as he would have liked it to be, produced his little book of poems. As we sat in front of the open fire with hot coffee and good old-fashioned rusks he read them to me:

This is one I wrote during my nine months National Service Training. You will have to excuse the language at times, but you know what soldiers in the bush are said to be like.

'Soldier's Lament'

Here we sit all four
With feet both tired and sore
On our faces not a smile
For we have walked many a mile.

When we are from camp we're not gay
For we have 'Stand to' both night and day
Every time we're stopped or bused
By either tsetse or mopani flies we're chased.

They say our graze for Kings it's fitting
But when we're stopped we commence to shitting
On first coming in we get nothing but jabs
But later we take nothing but camoquine and salt tabs.

With visions of tracks and water on the mind
We find that the Batonka's are very kind
Our water bottles are both empty
For water holes are far from plenty.

Far in the distance the gomo's (hills) just wind
With all our thoughts on or beds we find.
For onward eternal we seem to go
Praying to God we see no Foe

But like everything it come to an end
When we see playtime, our friend
At the end of patrol with our hearts full of cheer
We are always rewarded with a cold beer.

A thin tired smile appeared on my face. "That's good," I said, "Did you really write it?" "Yep," said Keith. "Do you want to hear another one?" "What is it about?" I said.

"It is about you. I wrote it while you were nursing." "Of course, I do." I said as I sat up looking more alive. "It has no name," Keith, confessed.

> I met a girl whose hair is gold,
> Whose heart is anything but cold,
> Her lips are always ever yielding
> But for only the one her hearts loudly beating.
>
> Into love with her I blindly plunder
> Now any heart beats sound like thunder.
> Upon my heart again ping!
> I will ask her to wear a wedding ring
> But until that happy day is nigh,
> I'll just be content to give a big sigh.
> For a total of three years she'll spend
> In a place that'll drive her round the bend.
>
> During her years she learns to cure
> All my monies in the bank; will procure,
> Oh but nothing could be finer.
> Then the love I have for 'Miss Miner'.

I was so embarrassed I dived under a cushion. To conceal my embarrassment I started to find fault with his poem. "My hair is not gold!" I said, "And anyway how did you know about Miss Miner?" Our servants had never been able to say Myrna so I had always been Miss Miner but knowing this not to be the case with Keith's servant he always managed to get round it by saying 'Bass Key's Madam.' Keith said, "I have heard the servants on the farm."

Keith then confessed that the night after meeting me at the Young Rhodesian's Social Club, I had been the topic of conversation at their breakfast table. His mother was very shocked when he walked out of his bedroom dressed and ready for breakfast so early on a Sunday morning. He then announced that he had met a girl he wanted to marry. Keith said he thought he had knocked the wind out of her sails.

She never had her usual 'eleventeen' cups of tea. I have never known anyone who could out drink Mrs. Seagrave when it came to tea.

You may as well read my other one, it too has no name Keith said as he left the room.

> Everything seems much brighter
> When I make her heart lighter.
> Every time, I send shivers up her spine
> I know for a fact that she is mine.
>
> No matter what moods we're in
> Upon seeing each other, we both start to grin.
> When we're both close and near,
> God my heart sends out a loud cheer.
>
> I used to yearn for cigarettes,
> I used to yearn—for beer.
> But all I yearn for now, my sweet
> Is for you to be so very near.

I put his book down as he walked into the room. Keith had been to make some more coffee. "There has been a horrific accident in Wankie," Keith said as he handed me my cup. "One of the shafts has collapsed, there was a news flash while I was in the kitchen. We will have to listen to the news at 7:45," Keith said.

Four hundred and sixty-five men were trapped after an underground explosion and cave-in at Wankie Number Two colliery. The explosion was thought to have been caused by methane gas. Carbon monoxide had seeped through the network of tunnels which extended over eleven miles and to a depth of nearly one thousand two hundred feet. This disaster has been mentioned in a report commissioned by the Swiss Federal Office of Energy in 1998 "Server Accidents in the Energy Sector" complied by Hischerg S.; Spiekerman G. And Dones R. Table 6.2.3

The horror of the Wankie disaster never had that much of an impact on us at the time. The full extent of the disaster reached its climax some weeks later when we were back in Salisbury. The newspapers relived the story through the women and families that were left. By 3:30 p.m. on the 9 June there were four hundred and twenty-six men still entombed and the fires were still raging underground. It was decided then that the risks involved in trying to recover the bodies were too great. The South African team of rescuers together with the Zambian and Nigerian teams abandoned the area. The shaft was then sealed. I was not the only one to cry river of tears on June 6, 1972.

I then thought how wrong our system was. The Africans culture allows them to have more than one wife. In our laws, it was wrong and not accepted. Some Africans, in fact many of them, were ashamed of their ways either for fear of ridicule or that they had been told they were breaking the law. The African male would only register his first wife responding to perhaps outside pressure in order to keep his job. Only when a disaster on this mammoth scale happens do we realise the full extent of the system break down. The women were traditionally less educated than the males. This was not only the case in their population but in some lower socioeconomic circles. I remember once when Adam asked me why the hell I could not achieve the high grades at school that Willy was bringing home, my mother said my marks did not matter as brains on a girl were wasted. While he made this comparison Willy was never praised for his achievements.

Women and children were sneaking out of the compounds at night because they were among the ones that were not on record as being the man's true wife and would therefore not be entitled to any compensation. The officials were quick to realise that these women were leaving without claiming full compensation. Times they were told to return to their homes. Some went back but many were just too frightened because they had never been properly educated in to our system. These women became an added burden to the lost husband's older, brother. That was one of the African customs—i.e., if Keith died, Mark, Allan, and I would become John's property. I would become his second or third wife depending on how many he had. Mark and Allan would be his sons. It would then be Mark's duty, as the oldest son, regardless of the fact that John has an older daughter than Mark to look after John and all his wives, in his old age. This usually meant that the oldest son would never have enough money to pay for his own wife until his father died leaving him all his worldly goods, these would include goats, cows and wives. Mark's mother would have a more special place in the home John's wife would now become number two in the family.

Our first home was a small council flat at Birchenough Court in Belvedere. My mother and stepfather began to take an interest, visiting us a few times. Several visits passed when Adam suggested that Keith could earn far more money working for a private company then the council. Keith applied for a position on Alaska Copper Mine in Sinoia.

Keith and I discussed the repercussions which may or may not come about with being so close to my parents. We decided to take the move in our stride and so in February 1973, we moved to Sinoia. The mine assured us that a small garden flat was available. When we arrived, we found ourselves in what was told to us the only available accommodation, a house immediately opposite my parents. After a dispute in June the same year, Keith and our little family moved back to Salisbury. My nightmares which were almost as common as sleep, ceased. Once again, I became content and at peace with myself. We lived in a caravan for a very short spell until a garden flat became available in Clyst Road in Hatfield. Our stay was not intended to put down roots. We moved from there to Edelweiss Farm until our house was built in Houghton Park.

The war, which was to last many years, had become part of our lives. To begin with, Keith did three camps a year during which time he missed so much of Mark's first two years. It was difficult for them to become best friends. Each time Keith returned home, he was more tanned; his eyes were hard and sharp, continually on high alert for anything out of the ordinary. His eyes were never relaxed, matching his nervous quick temper. Mark was always very bright so when this person approached him, he sensed Keith's inner insecurities and reacted the only way he knew how. Hiding behind me, he would look questioningly at Keith then retreat to his safe place me. The pained expression in Keith's eyes, sometimes resulting in temper outbursts, as Mark rejected him, this was easier to ignore and never mention. Mark, as I did grew to accept this as a way of life.

Following that first confrontation when Mark was just one, Keith realised he would have to live two separate lives. Keith displayed a tremendous amount of willpower, he calmed down, appeared the loving father to whom Mark always responded. Mark and Keith were inseparable. I remember the first time Mark walked over two miles in search of his daddy. The afternoons were very hot and most children were kept indoors, especially the very young, who spent an hour or two asleep. Over the weekends, Keith would take advantage of this. He would disappear for a few restful hours fishing. On Edelweiss, the dam was some two miles away from the main house. I too, like Keith, took advantage of the situation and retreated as I slept lazily. During our stay at Edelweiss, I was recovering from Bilharzia (my canal swimming days had caught up with me) the doctors said it manifested itself when my system was weakened by the miscarriage a few months earlier. Mark waited, biding his time, let the cot sides down and stole out the house. After his first Houdini attempt, we tied his sides up but he was a true escape artist. Making his way to the African Compound where he found many willing piccaninnies, he made them understand he wanted his daddy. He was only taken there once before. His love for his fishing and his daddy's company never allowed him his rest over the weekends.

Our house was completed, and in 1974, we moved to 492 Sandon Close. Keith made a name for our home, once the fence and gates were erected, we displayed our name plaque proudly Mapandus (Ma-Pa-and-us). Taking stock of my life, I had my very own house with two very special people and a third on the way. Keith hoped it would be a girl but my wish was for another son. A garden with as many flowers as animals, ducks, chicks, two tortoises who had the run of the garden, cats, and three dogs, and just so as not to forget where some say, we started from the water, a fish pond. Neptune's face overlooked the miniature waterfall as the water poured out of his mouth and flowed down in gentle ripples into a small pond. Large and small gold fish played in the turbulence at the bottom of the waterfall. The Japanese imperial carp hovered just beneath the leaves of a candy pink water lily.

Allan arrived in May 1975, and our family was complete. Allan and I had been home a few days when it was once again time for Keith to leave us. Our way of life was becoming a terrific mental strain. Many of my friends were on different drugs prescribed by their doctors. Listening to the news became almost an obsession which left you with such mixed feelings it was no wonder that some needed more than their willpower to see a day out. Hearing the news announcer say, "Here is an official communication" I secretly thought please don't let it be my loved one, then sighed with relief as I would thank God as I realized it was not. Almost in the same instant I would have a terrible feeling of guilt as I became aware that while sitting there, with bated breath, I had wished someone else dead. These feelings of guilt and confusion were getting stronger, at one point I refused to listen to the news. I too lapsed into moods of depression which I knew deep down would magically disappear upon Keith's return. Rhodesia had the highest divorce rate in the world during the 70s and 80s. This experts attributed this to, "war stress." I was very fortunate that Keith's homecoming was always like a second honeymoon. There was never anytime for petty fights. Our time together was far too short.

Keith returned two weeks sooner than he should have. Mark's godmother Phyllis Smyth died after a massive brain haemorrhage. She had slipped and fallen in the bathroom hitting her head on the basin. Working my way through the maze of army officials for an entire day, I contacted a very good friend who was in the Selous Scouts. Thankfully, it was one of those rare occasions he was home, he managed to locate Keith. At first, he was unsure whether he would be able make it home. Not having a telephone, he promised to phone a friend. Once I arrived, I found, to my disappointment, Keith had not phoned. Angry and disappointed, I decided to have a Sunday out. Monday was another day, and I could worry about the situation in the light of a new day. I felt restless and depressed. My weeks while Keith had been away had had that many pitfalls.

The phone had been struck by lightning. I was so lucky not to have been in the bedroom at the time. The phone was on my side table next to my side of the bed. The handset lay scattered in black moulted bits while the wires scorched the wall all the way to the ceiling. There was a very strong smell of Bakelite in the room from the old black phone. My new house's sewage had had a garden pick put through it which resulted in no water for three days; I had an attempted break in; the car's brakes failed, two weeks prior, when I took the TV into be repaired following a mishap with Mark. The garage noticed a noise in the engine always on the lookout for extra business took that to pieces, leaving me without a car. Unbeknown to Keith, he not telephoning had just added the fermented tomato sauce to my scrambled eggs. (That's another tale.)

Children find the most simplistic of things hilarious. Keith shook the tomato sauce bottle at the dinner table once. The top exploded off spraying sauce from the dining room to the fish tank in the sitting room. The walls were covered in the stuff. Mark almost fell out of his high chair, he was laughing so much. I just saw the mess. We had to laugh at Mark when he said, "Do it again, Daddy, do it again."

Returning from my day out, I found Keith exhausted, sawing an entire forest down. Mark woke his Daddy up saying, "One kiss for Teddy Fred, and now one for me." Keith made the mistake of asking why I had borrowed his Dad's car knowing how he objected. Besides which, they were very expensive items to fix should anything go wrong with it while in my care. My past four weeks were revealed in great detail with a foot note. I didn't want to play house anymore. Keith, showing his usual restraint saw to the sewage, reconditioned Little Stink's engine in the spare room. Then had the TV mended. He spoke to Geoff Blyth who was a lecturer at the Salisbury Polytechnic, he was considered 'essential services' so his 'call ups' were done in the police reserves about the attempted break-in. Geoff suggested we use the bush telegraph to our own advantage. Mrs. Gus still had the First

Battalion Rifle Range at Edelweiss. One weekend Keith asked David if he wanted to come to the farm with us. We would need him to look after the two children while Keith showed me how to shoot. Up till then while I carried an FN Automatic Pistol in my handbag there was no wide broadcast of its existence. We went out and I shot at and hit a two pound jam tin every time at 30 feet. Keith said that I was a regular Annie Oakley. David was silent, his eyes were wide with amazement all the time. I did not have the same success with the .22 rifle but I think the point had been made by then. Keith discovered I didn't have a dominant eye and consequently I would close the wrong eye when looking down the length of the weapon but we never had any more trouble with break-ins while Keith was away. Geoff suggested that the word had been sent out don't mess with that madam. She has a gun and knows how to use it. Keith solved everything and then added the cream to the final course. He bought me an eternity ring with his entire army pay.

His first day back at work had a reward that he deserved. His syndicate won the Arts and Sports Lottery—'Electrified' had won them eighty thousand dollars, each member received three thousand dollars. Keith sold our 1965 Anglia and bought a new Renault Six. We paid off the little outstanding accounts which the new house had brought about. Keith's winnings had also made us more aware of the more precious things around us.

Charlie duck's white neck was once more noticed, while he stood at the edge of the pond bathing his head and neck. Charlie and Matilda were both white Muscovy ducks. As women find their mate's weaker points, Matilda was no exception. Charles, I think, is the only duck in the world that didn't like water. He would stand on the side of the pond screeching and beating his large powerful white wings while stamping his red tinged webbed feet, obviously outraged with Matilda as she teased him, just swimming out his reach. She would glide near him then almost as if to say, "If you want me you will have to come into my bedroom." She would sail into the middle of the pond leaving a slight wake. Charlie though quite frantic with frustration just stood on the side screeching severe words of reprimand at her and she in turn enjoying his every outburst of temper glided sedately on the water though ever wary that he might just take the plunge. She never fully turned her back on him. We figured that Charlie must have had things his way at times because eventually we did have a batch of eggs. We acquired Matilda and Charlie from Mrs. Petie. She had them as pets but then the three ducks turned out to be a drake and two ducks. She said that they just eat and never lay any eggs. I found out from Daddy Fred and then read that Muscovy ducks only mate in water. They will lay a batch of anything from 12 to 15 eggs at the rate of one a day but it is only the last few which will hatch as they don't sit on their eggs from day one. Daddy Fred said we ought to mark the eggs and take the first one laid when there were two and so on until we thought she might stop laying. Daddy Fred enjoyed duck eggs for a while. I only ever baked with them, they have a very strong taste. Mrs Petie did not have a pond for them hence the reason she did not get any eggs. We allowed Matilda to sit on five, three of which hatched. Keith named them Inky, Pinky, and Plonky.

Mark found these very fluffy yellow little darlings irresistible. One day he waited until Matilda had left the nest to go for her daily bath. Watching her, he opened the gate and quickly picked up one of the ducklings. The duckling squawked raising the alarm, Matilda came flying out of the water making a loud menacing noise she flapped her wings while she chased Mark. In his haste to get away from her, he forgot the gate. I realised Matilda meant business. I opened the bottom half of the back stable door and ran out to Mark's assistance. Trying to explain to Mark, while he ran round and round the garden with Matilda in hot pursuit, that all he had to do was to put her baby down was not as easy as it should have been. The more I told him to put the ducking down the more he called back to me, "It's my duckling."

The garden boy joined in the chase by this time. He caught hold of Matilda and took her back to the run and closed the gate. This gave me just enough time to get the duckling off Mark before she flew over the four foot fence and was once again in hot pursuit. I picked Mark up and comforted him while he shouted, "Bad, Matilda, bad,

Matilda." She fussed over her duckling a while. Protectively she took it under her wing and returned to the run. I explained to Mark why Matilda had chased him and that he should never take her babies away again. Putting me in her place, I said I too would have chased anyone if they had taken my babies and just as Matilda had flown over the fence I too would not give up until I had retrieved what was mine. Mark remembers his encounter with Matilda fondly. At the time, it became a game with the garden boy when Mark would teasingly run off with his tools. He would chase Mark round and round the garden mimicking Matilda in sound and action.

Over the weekends, Keith would wake up in the small hours of the morning and taking just his keep net and two fishing rods, he would disappear on his motor bike to a prearranged fishing stop. Mark, Allan and I would follow once we had had our breakfast and packed a lunch, more often than not arriving before about ten o'clock. Just in time for a welcome bacon and egg roll which we had brought for Keith's breakfast. Mark was never accepting of this arrangement. He often asked if he could go with Keith at five in the morning. In due course, Keith gave in but he had said once before that Mark could go but when the time came we felt that he was far too small and often the weather cooler than we thought fit for a three-year-old. Mark, on the other hand, just felt betrayed. I woke up one morning around three o'clock and walking past Mark's bedroom, on my way to the toilet, I saw his light on. Mark was awake reading a book. "What's the matter, Mark?" I said. He replied, "My daddy won't leave me this time because I am sleeping!" Reassuring him, I said I wouldn't allow Keith to leave him but it was much too early to be awake. I tucked him in, kissing Teddy Fred and him I turned his light off. When Keith woke up at five, I told him about Mark reading. Keith rightly said we had better not lie to him again and went to wake Mark. His light was on once again. He was fully dressed with his book over his face fast asleep. His determination paid off. He caught the only fish that day, a one and half pound bream. Mark enjoyed many an early morning fishing trip with Keith. He was always sure to get Keith's promise, always reminding Keith that if he didn't take him, he would not sleep.

Fishing remained one of Mark's fascinations. At times it was not safe or convenient for Mark to go down to the lake, just a stone's throw away from the house, so he would be allowed to fish in our pond with a bent pin and string. Keith had it well stocked with little minnows which he used for live bait when he fished for bass. Mark was always very good and threw the gold fish and koi back if he ever caught them. Our house boy thought Mark was fantastic. He more often than not would offer to take Mark fishing especially towards the end of the month when his money was running out and a fish meal would not go amiss.

Once I had an offer for one of the tortoises, but by the time the conversation ended, the garden boy was under no delusions, both tortoises were mine and mine alone. No matter how tasty they were, he was not eating them. He went to great lengths to tell me that they were roasted alive on very hot embers and, once cooked, the shell was very easily split by prizing a thick bladed knife between the join in the shell. It was little wonder when one day he came rushing in, very excitedly to David with a tale. The Portuguese lady next door was trying to kill one of the tortoises. Enraged I went storming out. "What! The hell are you doing?" I shouted at her. Snatching her rake out of her hand I tried to break it in half. But having put so much energy into my temper I had no strength left. I threw it back into her garden. One appears to always learn the swear words first in any language. I picked up the odd word that she was shouting back at me. Furious at the very thought that she should try and kill one of my pets, I let rip with a string of Afrikaans. In the heat of our fight, I never realised the large crowd of Africans gathering, that is until I heard loud cheers of laughter. Looking round I noticed my servants standing at the back door almost crying, they were laughing so much. Picking up my tortoise, I stormed into the house. David my house boy later told me that she thought it was a wild one and said it was very good meat. We were never on very good terms but from then on I never spoke to any of them. Once my temper quietened, I could see the funny side and often smiled to myself when I would hear David tell his friends about how his madam swore at the Portuguese in Afrikaans. Drawing his cheeks in and forming a perfect circle with his lips he moved his tongue quickly in, and out making a hollow babbling sound breaking in with the odd word in Portuguese and Afrikaans. Then picking up an imaginary tortoise he stomped off. He summed it up exactly, a tremendous noise none of which made any sense. It must have appeared quite funny as neither of us understood the other one.

In August 1975, Keith had another call up to do and we decided that on his return in October we would spend the rest of the money on a holiday in Kariba. October was always referred to as Suicide Month. It was exceptionally hot with little or no rain, and the thought of just sitting at the pool side was very welcome. Kariba is in the same area as Mana Pools, though unlike Mana Pools, Kariba caters largely for the rich tourists. There are luxurious hotels and very expensive curio shops. Our week at Kariba Breezes (originally Venture Cruises) was fantastic.

Most days we spent at the pool with cold meats and salad lunches. Periodically dipping onto the pool as the hot sun baked down on us, we tanned our skin to a golden sun bed finish. From midday to late into the afternoon, the pool's crystal blue surface reflected the hot sun without the slightest ripple except when a large blue dragonfly dipped in, breaking the surface tension. Small circles grew gracefully larger, until they disappeared into the vastness of the pool.

Mark's eating habits puzzled and disturbed me for the first few days. He was content, lively, and alert, but apart from consuming more cold drinks than we ever thought possible, his only other meal was one chip off one of our plates and a small pile of salt. Through the entire meal, Mark sat sucking a very soggy chip after repeatedly dipping it into his salt pile. Only when I noticed that Allan too had gone off his food, leaving me rather uncomfortable, did I realise that both, boys were feeling the effects of the intense Kariba heat. Keith had a quiet word with the manager and a Mark's Special was invented. This was a milk shake, ice cream, one raw egg, flavouring, and milk. Mark thought he was very special having a drink named after him. The waiters too took great delight in bringing him his special glass, held importantly high as they wove their way through the many tables. The waiter then stood back, pleased that the piccaninny bass was eating more than a soggy chip. Some gave their words of encouragement while others suggested he try different flavours.

One morning we woke up very early and hired a boat. The vast expanse of water looked like a becalmed sea. Small islands of bright fresh green Kariba weed dotted the water. In places these islands grew so dense and solid they could stop a small power boat dead. If one was silly enough to venture through the middle of it. Kariba weed was the name given to Salvinia Auriculata it was introduced from its native land Brazil, for the expectation of controlling the Bilharzia snails Lake Kariba was not only intended as a hydro electric power supply but also a tourist attraction, which would involve a number of water sports. The idea of a Bilharzia free aquatic plant was very quickly taken up but soon proved to be a menace. Kariba weed took over large sections of the dam very quickly, later a small species of fish was introduced which solely lived off the roots of the weed. It was hoped this would curb its growth rate. They were introduced and very quickly procreated and their numbers grew but then the Africans realised that they could net these little fish; Kapenta was a supplement to their diet.

Our day's fishing ended at midday without 'even the one that got away' tale to tell. It was common practice to have the chef, cook one's Kariba bream for dinner, after one of the other kitchen hands had cleaned your fish but as we had an empty keep net we settled for steak and salad.

From four o'clock until sunset a large boat cruised around on Lake Kariba capturing exquisite sights of the many different animals coming down to the shore line for their final drink of the day. Seeing these animals one couldn't help but remember Operation Noah. Some experts felt that as the islands submerged with the rising water level the animals, being intelligent creatures would seek drier islands. The opposite happened. They became frightened, confused, and dangerous. Rupert Fothergill, one expert, seeing the plight of the animals, set up Operation Noah. In a very hectic six months, between March and September 1959, racing against the rapidly rising water, Fothergill saved one thousand two hundred animals. By the completion of the operation some thirty-five species, totalling five thousand animals were saved.

To begin with, the Batonkes wouldn't accept their relocation settlements. It appeared that the River God did not like the idea of the river being dammed either. Severe floods damaged many coffer dams. Work began in 1955 but in 1957 early heavy rains flooded the coffer dams. Work was still hampered in 1958 by severe floods, the Africans insistent that Nyaminyami, their River God, (half fish——half snake) was angry and that Kariba would never be completed. Kariba was paid a royal visit on May 16, 1960 when Queen Elizabeth the Queen Mother declared it open. The Batonkes became reconciled as did Nyaminyami, the animals also settled into their new environment.

I once read a book and was angry when the man wrote only about the hundreds of animals that were killed by the flood waters of Rhodesia when Kariba was built. Perhaps I should make allowances for him, coming from Europe. It is only when disasters like the Ethiopian famine strike do outsiders begin to question the non development of other countries. Rhodesia has at least tried to make the most of her rivers and in the long term saved more than the initial five thousand. The people who died during the building of such a project died so that their descendants would have a more prosperous life. Unlike during the last World War, I argue, those were needless deaths. Some eighty-year-olds would also wonder "Why did they survive, only to be mugged for a meagre few pounds that they earn once a week?"

During our week we spent some time at the large crocodile farm, fascinated by the prehistoric reptiles, basking in the sun on the mud and cemented banks. I disagree with animals, especially wild ones, being kept solely for slaughter, to accommodate human vanity. We never dwelt on the thought of any of them in relation to ladies handbags but just enjoyed their unique ugliness, finding Keith's army term 'Flat Dogs' very appropriate.

In the evenings, Keith would often go into the bar and have a few games of darts. This particular time a very outgoing South African approached him and asked him why his daughter was so stuck up, he had been trying to get my attention all day and I would not have a bar of it. Keith said, "Perhaps that is because she is my wife." Poor Keith this was the second time he had been mistaken for my father.

The first was while I was nursing someone came down to the old night quarters to say my father was here to see me. It was not common but from time to time he did turn up like the proverbial lost penny. I walked out into the foyer and not expecting to see Keith and looking a little confused when this voice said, "Oh, you don't know me today." Without thinking that someone would think Keith was my father there is only four years between us I just blurted out, "I was told my dad was here to see me."

Our South African made amends by taking Keith and me to the casino. Never having an abundance of money, I was very wary of gambling and watched at a distance most of the night. Well into the evening, Keith persuaded me to play a game on the roulette table. Changing seats with Keith, I took my place. Keith and our friend were so engrossed with their scheming of which was the best way to play. I on the other hand, having not taken as much interest as perhaps I should have, kept asking, "which number can I put it on?" The number twenty-eight came out of their conversation so on it went. My next question, "Keith, how much can I put on?" No reply. The wheel spun round. "Last bets, place your last chips now, please," echoed the croupier's voice. "Keith," I said, "Is this alright?" Keith bent down and as he did I whispered, "My number is going to come up, you watch, could I have put more money on it?" "You are better not to, you didn't want to lose it all at once." He said, lacking my confidence. As the wheel grew slower and slower, the little white ball bounced round, first landing in the black, then red, finally settling nicely in twenty-eight. The croupier pushed a large pile of chips towards me. I pushed them back to her saying, "I want my money!" The entire table collapsed laughing. "Please!" I added hastily. Passing it back to me, she said, "You have to collect your money from over there, pointing towards the sign that said Cashier. Collecting my piles, I gave Keith a handful and pointed him towards the cashier. My lucky number paid forty to one. Keith said that I was very lucky. I then said, "Well, not really, you told me to put it on twenty-eight." "No, I did not!" replied Keith. "Yes, you did. When I asked you which number could I put it on, I heard you say twenty-eight!" replying quite positively. "You were very lucky indeed, I was saying that I have a system by which I cover twenty-eight numbers at once, that way I ensure myself of winning something most times!" Keith said laughingly. Our evening ended at half past two, when we walked out of the air conditioned casino. My forty dollar dream ended abruptly the reality of the heat blanketed us, as we stepped outside into a clear dark night. Our casino evening is often recalled amongst our other happy times.

Allan was almost 8 months old and had not been christened yet. I have a confession. This was mostly my doing. I did not want him to wear the christening robe. He was a little boy, dresses were for girls. The other part of this was trying to fit family things in however important they might be when your husband was only home for ten days was almost an impossible task. I eventually found the local Church of England Church and after some stern exchange of words with the minister had Allan christened. His argument was that I was not a member of his congregation and because of this he felt he was not able to christen Allan. Not being a very regular church person, I quoted something which I had read once which went something like "suffer all little children unto me" and ended the quote with I don't recall it saying anywhere that the parents had to be a member of any church. I did go to church for two consecutive Sundays while Keith was in the bush and then set the Sunday aside which we expected Keith to be home.

Tiny and Ken Newing were asked to be his godparents. We also asked Charlie Matheson's wife June. I had noticed something with Allan right from very tiny he never liked to be nursed and fussed. Nowadays, this behaviour would be associated with Autism but back in the 70s we just accepted some kids loved to be cuddled while others did not. I was not a very cuddly person. In fact, I would stiffen up quite rigidly if someone whom I did not know tried to get too close to me, like mother, like son. June was one person Allan had a very difficult time with. He just screamed and screamed if she held him.

Allan was a biter. I once read that children who bite are very clever and the reason they bite is they see no need to get into what might be a lengthy conversation. If you bite another person they will drop whatever they have, and at that point, you can retrieve it; easy! The treatment way back in the dark ages as my son now calls it was to bite the child back, which I did many times. This never worked with Allan. The number of times he bit Mark, I had lost count. One day, all three of us were sitting in the spare room on a large sheet of plastic working out of a Lady Bird Book. It had small crafty type projects. Mark was making his Gran a papier-mache flowerpot. Allan was painting old cotton reels to make his snake. The next second Allan got up walked around me and bit Mark square on the top of his shoulder. Mark let out an almighty whelp and instantly turned on Allan and bit him on his arm and said, "There, now you see it hurts, so stop it!" Allan was so taken aback he just stared at him. I am not sure if it was the reference to the fact that it hurt or whether it was at the point that Allan was naturally going to stop biting but he never bit Mark or any other person again.

Foster Parents

It is very difficult, thinking back. Why did we all accept the way we lived? It's not difficult to see why our family went to pieces when Adam died. My mother, for the first time in her life perhaps, was free. She was her own boss. The younger children were free! With so much freedom, they had been like caged animals set free. Living life to the extreme, they all had a lot of time to make up. No longer under Adam's tyranny, they had many things to do and many areas to explore. I experienced this newfound freedom when I met Keith he would say, "Don't do that that way you will get hurt." I would reply, "Please, let me find out for myself."

I put no blame on my mother or the children, it was just circumstances. I had put forward a proposed plan which was rejected outright. Social Welfare called some time later to say as Gretha was to leave school at the end of the year, and unlike me, she was not a ward of the court but once she had turned 16 was no longer the concern of Social Welfare. Gretha too was going through a particularly bad period. So much talk of her going blind before being able to complete her schooling was very unsettling and being moved from one foster home to another did not help. My brother not being in Rhodesia at the time, it was, I thought, up to me to try and do what had to be done. Gretha, always being my soft spot and appearing on the surface slightly more conscientious, was my main concern following the call from her case worker.

Keith and I talked it over and eventually in 1967 went to Bulawayo, where my mother was staying at the time. We collected Gretha. The other two children asked what about us I said well, you are still at school. Once you have finished school, we will sort something out for you as well. Shortly after Gretha arrived, I found that never again would she allow anyone to have a hold on her. Providing she was allowed to come and go, do her homework when and if she pleased, things remained very smooth on the surface with a very turbulent under current. I, knowing what a strict upbringing we had had found her very difficult to deal with, her tempers and outbursts were very regular.

Keith was always the control, he never took sides with either of us but said we were typical sisters, always at one another. Gretha lived with us for two years and although her eyesight deteriorated, she only lost the sight of one eye. Through even the most heated outburst she never once threatened to leave home. We discussed becoming her legal guardians but Gretha had such strong views about being someone's possession that we never followed the idea through.

Her final action, proving to us that she was going to be an individual came when we presumed that she would leave Rhodesia with us. Neither of us listened to her. We took it for granted that when the time came, she would leave, follow us like a lamb.

Sometime during 1978, Keith and I applied for emigration status for Australia. It wasn't until we actually heard Gretha telling our interviewer she had no intentions of leaving Rhodesia, did it sink in. Keith was cross, I was hurt. To think that we had put in so much effort into showing her a different and gentler life, I felt Gretha ought to be more appreciative. I had been a foster child and as such went along with every idea regardless. We both felt very let down. I tried to put across that she had missed a one-off chance. If indeed she wanted to, at a later date, she could always return to Rhodesia. Gretha remained adamant she was not going to leave. Due to the internal family disagreement, we failed our interview. In June 1979, Gretha completed a secretarial course at Salisbury Polytechnic and said she wanted to branch out on her own. Social Welfare assisted us and Gretha moved in the YWCA in Salisbury. Initially, I felt very hurt and refused to visit Gretha. Then it suddenly became clear. Gretha was only doing what every child would do. She had left home just as I did when I got married. Her first settling-in period would be more difficult for her than it was for me. On my way home from work one evening, I popped in. I hoped I had prepared myself for any tension or awkwardness. My fears were alleviated we were the best of mates

After my first visit, Gretha invited me to tea and in turn she came home for the odd weekend. Keith and I, I thought, survived as foster parents not making too serious a mistake. Several years later when Gretha's letters arrived she admits that we were her best foster parents and says thank you. Gretha's stay with us caused a large rift between the family. I was 26, I had my own children, and our pending move was taking place.

Good-bye Rhodesia

We had managed to sell our little house in Houghton Park by 1978. We were now living in Greendale. Mark was exceptionally happy at Courtenay Selous Junior School. The war was intensifying. Many men spent six weeks in the army and ten days at home. Everyone was nervous, children were being abducted, mainly African children but also a small portion of European children. Words and phrases like *'convoy, kill a ter for me'* were becoming commonplace. It was also, when all is said and done, it was our home and because of this we told ourselves it would be different tomorrow. The tomorrows never came.

At one point I said to Keith, "One day Mark and Allan will think that there is no other way to life besides the one in which you have to kill your fellow man just to survive. We in Rhodesia will breed a generation of kids just like they have in Ireland. Those kids don't even know why they are fighting but do so because their parents did. We owe it to the boys to show them that there is another side to life. A side to life where you are not searched every time you go into a shop, where a weapon is not a part of you, where we don't check our possessions in the order of weapon, deodorant, and comb." After an entire year of 'what if, buts, and may be' did I decided to leave Rhodesia as so many others were doing.

We arrived in the UK on the 13 December 1979. I had lived there for five years, when I came to the conclusion that although I think of Rhodesia as my Utopia there is no such place. Rhodesia had problems, its advantages and disadvantages, but then so does any other place in the world.

I never asked myself why did we leave Rhodesia even during our most difficult times I never said, "Why did we leave?" That is until in the morning at twenty to six on April 2 1985. I had spent a very restless night on the flight to Zimbabwe. I looked out the little double glazed windows. What a spectacular sight! Slightly confused, I was fixated at what looked like dark dunes in the near distance. Which desert would it be? Then realizing the time it was not desert it was the clouds. The sky looked like a lake changing from almost black nearest the plane to bright deep orange towards the horizon fading slowing into a paler black, and in places pink. The horizon changed again into deep blue to the extreme left. The airy lake immediately in front of me was marked with grey misty black islands of clouds. Raising through the dunes a shimmer, a road? No, it was the Congo River. Like a great fire ball rearing out of the horizon, intensely round, its circle fading with its own light. Dawn had broken——six a.m.

Oh God, what made me leave such a spectacular continent? The cloud dunes were a pale misty grey blue and motionless, like solid vegetation islands. Six twenty-five. The ball of fire burnt brightly, so intense was its light it changed its colour no longer. The bright deep orange was now like a ball of phosphorus. It changed the dunes to blinding white snow with bright blue rivers and lakes emerging through the snow desert.

I lost track of the time as I stared out of the window. I thought of Keith and the two boys in the UK. I felt my eyes begin to cloud matching my melancholy mood. I shook myself and thought of the welcoming reception that was waiting for me at Harare airport. Mrs. Gus and Gus were the first to pick me out of the crowd as we stepped off our plane. Standing at the top of the gangway, I paused a moment and looked around. Once I was on the tarred runway I thought I should look back at the silver bird that had flown me so many miles. Yet as I did, I still had no inner feelings of, "Oh, it's great to be home" as I had so often felt when I had lived in Rhodesia and returning from a holiday. My trip to Zimbabwe was just another journey and another stage in my life which I had to, pass through to arrive at the next stage. I wonder will that inner feeling that sense of belonging ever return or am I to be lost forever.

Part Two—Growing up in England

I have called this sequel "Growing up in England" because that is truly where I "grew up". I remember going to a gynaecologist after having had a miscarriage and two children at the tender age of 23 and wanting to be sterilized and he said, "Young lady, go away and come to me when you are 35 and have grown up." As I sat there, I felt most indignant. I thought to myself, "You sod, I am grown up. I have two children." I then said to him, "It's alright for you to talk. You have a salary that can afford 9 children, given my track record I am going to be having a baby every year because I can't take the pill. His reply was that there are many religious orders who forbid women to take the pill.

After spending ten years in England, I knew what this man meant. I had not grown up, had no real life experiences. Adam while he most definitely insisted that we had table etiquette, denying us any friends, we never got the ideas he was so worried about but then neither were we world wise. My own boys are quite amused at how naive I am. When they tell jokes I have to sit and try and work them out in my mind. My expectations of England were that we spoke the same language and most of all I had come from a country which was colonised by the British. This meant for me we would have a similar outlook on life. Wow, was I in for an enormous culture shock! My most significant life experience in England was one of prejudices. I had never been on the receiving end of this very destructive human failure. I had been able to hide behind my own prejudices if I indeed had any by telling myself I was not racist, I just choose not to mix with certain people. I would for instance not mix with someone who was foul mouthed regardless of their colour or religion. These points were not a factor because that was how it was. I remember one Christmas when the Villagers climbed on to a trailer and went round singing Christmas carols to everyone, we collected money for one charity or another. We came to one of the stately homes and were sent round to the back of house through wet, muddy and cow smelling entrance. Our carol was short lived as we were told the master of the house was not quite ready for us. We stood and waited in silence for the Master! He arrived and we started up. The carol was not too his liking, it was stopped. A new one which he liked was started. One verse into the carol he walked inside and just left us standing. I was so angry and thought back to our days we were entertained on the farm, was this how the Africans felt while entertaining us, were we wrong.

I remember my childhood days when living with Adam and him saying the English were White Kaffirs. As a child, I remember being horrified at this remark and thought how wrong it was to call another white person that. So perhaps in those thoughts, I was racist. This being so, what makes a person is not just the colour of their skin, a whole heap of factors including and most of all their own mind set go into making up a human being, who they are and what choices they make in life.

To best put my point across is to tell you of my experience of how I matured and grew up. When we first arrived in England in December 1979, we stayed with Keith's half brother. This fact was to come home to me some years later because he was never referred to by any of Keith's family not even Keith as a half brother. John collected us from Heathrow Airport. The journey was to take another 4 or 5 hours to Uttoxeter. Along the highway, satellite towns have been developed. One such place is Milton Keynes. We stopped along the road at once such place to refresh and have a toilet break. As we walked along the corridor, a man mopping the floor commented on the weather. Keith replied. John pulled Keith aside and just loud enough for me to hear he said, "If you want to get on in England, you don't talk to the likes of that!" Keith and I just looked at each other not a word was said about the subject. Sometime later, I asked Keith what was that all about. He said, "Well, you know John, if the person is not stinking of money he would not cross the street to piss on him if he was on fire." I accepted this as John being a snob. We spent our first Christmas with John and his family in Uttoxeter. It was our first experience of snow. We all loved it. Mark and Allan ran bare foot in the snow. The bare foot practice soon changed but not the fun. Snow has a certain magic to it. I still feel that sense of joy and wonderment when I look at Christmas cards, they portray the magic and fun which appears to be had by the picture people I hold on to this dream-like state for a moment as I hold old and new cards in my hand even today, 17 years later.

In the New Year, we moved briefly on to Keith's mother's brother, Uncle Clifford, who lived in Dalby. We were introduced to the Lady of Long Clawson's Manor, Alice Wilfred. We had arrived in the village Keith was born in. His parents had left for the greener pastures of the colonies. Keith made a lasting impression on a number of the older folk in the village. He had his third birthday on the boat which brought them out to Africa. We were at a village function once and a little old lady came up to Keith and said, "I know you, you are Fred Seagrave's lad" and slapped him saying that is for all the times you stole my milk.

The story goes that Keith would watch as the milk men put the glass pint, half pint and third pint bottles of milk on each of the terrace house's steps. Some would get two bottles while others only one and then a lucky minority would get three. Keith saw the unfairness of this and shared the bottles out equally along the row of terrace houses, making sure that they were shared equally according to size and number for each household. For months, no one was able to work out what was happening to their milk delivery. We were told he had a flare for some choice words at the tender age of two as he watched the black ants march along the bakery shop window where he would command all to look at the 'Little Black Buggers."

Despite this history, we were foreigners right up to when we left some ten years later. I never understood this fact. Keith has cousins, auntie, and uncles through the surrounding villages and Nottingham. At family functions, we were either introduced or people would remark, I know you and that lad must be your son, he is the spitting image of you but who does that one belong to. I was quite astounded by their rudeness. Allan did look a lot like Keith in his younger days, curly blonde hair and blue eyes. Mark was more like me, while he had light hair it was not the curly Seagrave head, it was straight and very fine, though not unlike and that different to Keith one could not see the family resemblance. I often thought if they gave their brain half a chance before they engaged their mouth one would have to assume that as we all walked in together we were a family. Keith always at that point thought he was being ever so clever and tried to break the ice with, "Well, the doc did work out the time he was conceived I was in the bush." I would always return with "What a shame all our milk men are black so he is clearly not the milk man's son!" I pulled Keith up about it once and said I was having a very difficult time relating to these people and he was not making it any easier. He said but have you noticed how quickly they shut up. This did not make it any easier for me, I was always bothered by what people thought and said about me.

Alice lived in the manor house which was said to have been around in Oliver Cromwell's day. The Manor House is situated on the opposite corner to the Anglican Church. There was always said to be a tunnel from the manor house to the church which Alice disputed all the time we live in Long Clawson. Elsie, Keith's Dad's sister, in her youth cleaned the Manor House and was sure the entrance to this tunnel was in a particular room's fireplace. Elsie said that this particular fireplace's hearth never did shine no matter how much polish she put on the floor and was sure it was because of the damp coming up through the floor.

When the Canadian Air Force withdrew from Langar Aerodrome after the last World War, Alice acquired two caravans. The two vans were put side beside and had a small kitchen area built as you entered and an area which was to be my sitting room for the first nine months of our life in England. Never really understood why Alice had seen the need to acquire the vans but was told many new families started their life off in these two caravans.

Perhaps much like the older style Queenslanders, which had their beautiful verandas closed in to accommodate sons returning from the war, England also had many more men return from the war than they had living quarters for.

Alice was a shrewd business woman. Perhaps she saw this as a means of building up her network of favours. To have a network of people on demand when you were a woman living alone in an aging house was excellent. Alice never took money for the use of the caravan but said her philosophy in life was a favour for a favour. Keith was never happy with this arrangement. Alice had a certain way with her 'favour for a favour' and exploited it to its fullest. Something we were to be held to for ten long years while we lived in the village. Many days a week, I would be seen in her garden weeding and cleaning up. I enjoyed this part of my favour being an avid gardener myself.

Alice also had a huge compost pile where all the weeds and grass clippings were piled. This pile was regularly set on fire. The villagers complained bitterly, as she had a way of starting the bon fire just as they would have white washing on the line and the wind blow in the right direction away from her home onto the council estate. After a few years of helping out in her garden, I was given permission to help myself to the charred remains of her compost mound. Keith said you know this is just going to tie you to her for longer. I was happy the soil was so rich and it saved me buying in top soil for my postage stamp. I built up a small veggie garden and carted 26 barrow loads of soil some 500 hundred yards from the manor house to 6 Kings Road, one Easter weekend. Keith was muttering under his breath each time it was his turn to push the barrow. We had the best spuds, gem squash, and the like that first year.

I never fully realised what a safe haven the caravan really was, not until many years later when I worked out for myself the social structure of the English. While we lived in the caravan, people who wanted to be seen with the right type of people could and would interact with us. They were able to talk to someone who was well spoken therefore the assumption was made we would be home owners. Our financial circumstances were that we could no more own our home as fly to the moon. The British people like things including the populace to be in nice tidy little boxes. They as a nation feel very comfortable to be able to say you fit here and you fit there and never the twain shall meet. A poem that I had to recite as a school kid epitomizes them if I am not mistaken a British chap wrote it. It was about two men who found themselves ship wrecked on an island and one day they discovered each other but as there was no one to introduce them to each other and because of this they did not know what each other's social standing was they went their separate ways and never did speak to each other again. The British, by nature, have to be right and proper. We did not fit into a category. They could not place us into a little box, and if they ever did, we were just too damn stupid or something was certainly wrong with us because we never stayed there.

The educated people lived in their own homes not council houses. To explain, Britain is very much a socialist state, and as such, it is the duty of the government of the day to provide each and every person a roof over their head. The population demand this as part of their rights. The wages are very poor. In 1980, in Rhodesia between us we earned a thousand dollars a month and at that stage the dollar was almost worth an English Pound. Keith was earning 67 Pound a week and the average house cost eighty thousand to buy. Hence, many council houses exits, unlike in Australia where the ratio of houses owned out right and those owned by government is a mere handful. Educated people, which means also well spoken people, because if one is educated one would have a high command of the English language which would ultimately provide them with very good paying jobs and would then provide them their own homes. They become Home Owners. The average Joe Citizen who was considered not well educated and did not fit into the Home Owner's Box lived in a Council House. Especially in villages, towns, and cities one would only see isolated pockets of this 'Boxing' type of life.

It is so prevalent there is even a different terminology for the two types. For some bizarre reason, a person who might live in a council house always lives in a house while the others live in a home. There is that suggestion that one person is capable of making a house into a home while the other has no idea and just never gets it right. We were brought up with the expectation that as you went to school so you strived to achieve the highest possible standard you were capable of achieving and if your talents where such that university was achievable; 'Good on you, Mate.' Nevertheless, if you were not capable of this standard this factor alone did not preclude you from being a Home Owner. It might be just a simple thing as your choice. In Britain, there did not appear to be a choice factor. Rhodesia was very much like Australia because we appear not to hold a stigma against the person who moved up the ranks. An example of this was Mr. Klette who started off his career as a math's teacher advanced to be a math's inspector of schools to eventually becoming the secretary to the Minister of Education. We here, in Australia, would now say he has done well for himself. In Britain, the remark was 'he has jumped up and should know his place'. Sadly, I never did know my place and if I did have a place there I was not very happy with it.

Before we left Rhodesia, Keith had to apply for leave from not only work but the Army he was attached to First Battalion, Infantry. Most people leaving discovered ways and means to secure whatever money they could to start a new life. We for two reasons bought return tickets. One, we were allowed to take out of the country a holiday allowance of a thousand Rhodesian Dollars each for the adults. This was doubled because we had not had a holiday overseas within the previous two years. The children were allowed 500 each and that too doubled. The second reason, I had been plagued with pneumonia from as old as three months, would I be able to take the British cold winters? Keith left us in February 1980 and did not return until just before Mark's birthday in April. Unfortunately, trying to buck the system left us in a position where we were only allowed one hundred and twenty pounds, this was considered our 'settling in allowance.' Ian Smith had one of the best foreign exchange policies in the world. We moved from the caravan in late September of 1980.

Both children and I lived a British winter in the caravan. It was so cold and damp the blankets froze to the side walls on the nights we forgot to move the beds away from the walls. One day, one of the boys had to crawl under their bed to find the elusive shoe that has a habit of sneaking off and hiding. He came out from under the bed breathless with excitement saying, "You know what, Mommy, I know where snow is made, it is growing under our bed!" Both boys were convinced that the snow was made under their beds. I never had to think about condensation running down the walls keeping the carpet constantly damp encouraging white mildew to grow. Realizing this spore was no good for any of us, I had a ritual every morning of drying the inside walls down and opening up as many windows as I could, most had been nailed shut to try and keep out some of the draft. Alice thought I was quite mad as all the Brits closed up everything as tight as they could. Those who could not afford double glazing found ways and means of insulating the windows, one such way was to stretch Glad Wrap over the windows after nailing them shut. I was opening up every door and window.

There was a great deal of things I had never had to consider. One day, Mark who hated England so much right from the start wrote to his primary teacher at Courtney Seloue. In his letter, he told Miss Jermaine, "After my birthday, I am coming home to Zimbabwe." Being the very practical person that I am, I was sure the right thing to do was to put him straight. Something I was later to give more thought to, he was only 6 was it that important to put him straight after all is our entire life not about dreams? We both sat on the bed and cried as I explained we were never to return to live in Zimbabwe. Mark never sent his letter but did not give up his dream either. One day, I looked for Mark around the caravan. It had started to snow and Mark was nowhere to be seen. I put my coat on and went outside. There was Mark with a hammer, nails, and bits of timber.
"Mark, what are you doing, it is too cold to be outside now, son."
"I am building a raft."
"You are not going to sail that thing on Alice's Pond!"
"No," he said, "I am going to sail it home to Zimbabwe!"

My heart went out to him as I walked quietly back inside, marvelling at how clever he was. We had travelled most of the long journey to England during the night but he knew he had crossed water to get to England and that was his way home. I think the cold got to him. He eventually abandoned his project for a warmer caravan. Zimbabwe was never far from his thoughts. One evening as they sat in front of the little seventeen inch black and white TV, having a warm drink

before bed there was a news flash. The Iranian Embassy siege had just happened. Mark sat with his mug half way to his mouth and just stared at the TV. When the drama had unfolded and the TV returned to normal viewing Mark turned around to look at me.
"Where is London?"
"In England."
"We live in England now hey, Mommy. Why did we leave Zimbabwe, they are killing people here too?"

I tried to make light of it. I did not really know the answer to his question. I said something like, "Mark, that is a long way away from us and it is not a real war not like in Zimbabwe and your daddy will not be called away to fight the Terrs." I felt as though my argument melted away as does a child's sand castle with the rising tide on a lonely deserted beach front.

Our thoughts, from the time we left Rhodesia was to use Britain as a stepping stone into Australia. It was very important to be very frugal with whatever money we had. We set our sights on a council house. The little house was just perfect. We scraped off years of wallpaper and replaced it with new fresh colours which reminded me of the wonderful sun and complete freshness of Zimbabwe. The kitchen where we were to spend many cold nights wrapped in blankets looking at our little black and white TV was now a bright pattern of small blue and white tile like shapes. The entire house was taking on a Seagrave look. The caravan was soon a distant memory. People to whom I thought I had forged a solidarity with began to painfully fade into the distance. In the village of thirteen right angled bends, everything you would consider life saving and absolutely necessary was within walking distance. The post office was the focal point for many to meet, chat, and continue on their way. As I adopted this daily ritual, I became more aware that a lady whom had befriended me, played badminton with me on Tuesday market days in Melton Mowbray found it very difficult to look at me as she grunted or mumbled her "good mornings." I came home and said to Keith I am not sure what I have done wrong to Chris, but it is almost as if she does not want anything to do with me. I relayed my experience to Keith his advice was that of 'Oh well, if you know you have done nothing to upset her then it is her problem." For me it was my problem. Why did she drop me like yesterdays cold mash potato? The encounters became more and more awkward until one day she crossed the road and walked on the opposite side so as to avoid greeting me. Diana and Jeff were new owners of the post office. They had recently arrived from Nottingham. City Folk as the villagers called them. I had not realise what a profound impact Chris was having on me because by the time I had arrived at the post office my eyes had welled up and Diana said, "Are you alright?" I explained my initial relationship with Chris and said she has just crossed over on to the opposite side of the street so as not to have to greet me. I also explained no one walks on that side, there is no foot path and with that steep embankment it was not safe, one has nowhere to go if a car comes round the corner. Jeff who had been packing shelves and being totally inconspicuous said, "You really don't know." I said, "Know what?" He explained Chris has to keep up her appearance you are a Council Tenant she is a Home Owner, she can't be seen with you anymore. He explained an experience he had when he was the local milk man. The lady of a certain house on the hill in the village he originally came from would chat, have a morning cup of tea with him as he delivered milk year in and year out but would not give him the time of day in the street. I said but that is just crazy. I am the same person today as I was 9 months ago when we lived in the caravan. "No, you are not. You made a choice to live with the lower class. I was not of her social standing and had to know my place." 'Know my place' my blood boiled and still does at that phrase. I tried to change the entire world with my one statement where a person lives does not make them one class or another, we are all human beings and command and should be given the same respect. Sadly, Britain has endured many years of the class system, and it is going to take many years and many people to change their ideology. Many City Folk have their roots in small villages because cities were once small villages and this idea is entrenched in them but where they score is they have met a number of travelled people and they themselves may have travel to the city once; they travelled from the small mindedness of a village. This incident, while I could not understand it, upset me so much that I would do anything so as not to venture out of my house for the next six weeks.

While Keith worked at the local dairy, one of the workshop floor managers was moved up the ranks, blue collar to a white collar worker. As he moved, so was he told his outlook towards his fellow work colleagues had to take on a new stance. He was told by upper management once he moved out of the workshop, he had to put a tie on and he was no longer to talk to or associate with the mechanics on the shop floor. If he needed to speak to anyone of them, it was to be done in his office and it was to be only about official business. Keith approached Mick at one of the renowned dairy annual dinners. Men appear to be able to be a lot more forthright than women. For most men, their life is black or white. Grey is not a part of their world not to the extent that grey is to a woman's world. Some men live their entire life as black or white. I know Keith's world is very black or white. Keith always got on very well with Mick and considered him a friend so when he moved and no longer acknowledged Keith, he asked him straight out what was the problem. Mick told Keith what his orders were. In hindsight, his way of handling his situation was far better. It was over and done within a matter of one conversation. Keith did acknowledge that while we lived in the UK, he would not be a manager as he would not take orders from any civilian. His days of taking orders were done the day he finished with the army.

I remember Christine my next door neighbour once telling a manger to 'get fucked' and not ever to approach her again. All year he can't even say thank you for the cup of tea she makes him and then come the annual dairy dinner, he wants to act like a human being. Christine was the Tea Lady at the dairy. Keith and I were shocked beyond words. We were not accustom to women using foul language but the next day Keith, congratulated her and said, "Well done, we all think that but none of us had the guts to say it." She admitted it was the booze which loosened her tongue and went on to say that is why her husband Roy would not attend any of these functions, because all year the very people who look down their noses at them now want to cross the floor and make out they are all one happy family.

During our stay in the village, Elsie told me that I was making a bad name for myself associating with my next door neighbour and I replied, "Well, at least I can count on Christine. I would not be able to count on the likes of Chris to come over and lend a hand in the middle of the night when I needed to be transferred to Leister Royal Infirmary in the back of an ambulance." Our Local GP had prescribed Codeine Hydroxcin (DF118) after a carpel tunnel procedure on my right hand, which resulted in me having drug induced fits. Christine may not have the elocution in the English language, she might only be 'The Tea Lady' at the local dairy, but she has a good heart and would not see her fellow man lie bleeding and dying in the street. She would cross over on to the opposite side so as to get involved. I will not change my friends to suit others opinions of me. I can't. I have to answer to myself every day. Elsie never realised but that conversation drew me out of my comfortable home. Chris could go to blazers, Keith was right, it was her problem. She later showed us how shallow she really was. Keith became the Scout Leader for the First Vale of Belvoir (pronounced Beaver) Scout Group. Shortly before we left Britain, they arrived at our doorstep with a gift for Keith and said this is for the Scout Master's wife. They would not come inside but just stood awkwardly at the front door. We thanked them. Keith and I acknowledge that obviously it was alright for them to be seen at our front door giving the Scout Master and his wife a parting gift.

I enjoyed being a part of my kids' life whether it was at school or in their social life. I got involved. This was a promise I made to myself as it was something I despised about my parents. They did not show their kids many considerations. We were objects, not people, and as an object if my stepfather choose to put us on a chair in a certain place that was his right and we were never able to have an opinion. In England I realised why I was always at loggerheads with him. I was always quite headstrong and because I had an opinion and wanted to share and express it. My children were going to have an opinion, I was going to have an opinion, and after all I was grown up now! Sadly with children having an opinion, adults have to be mature and have a mindset which is able to deal with this freedom they give children. I did not have this skill. I saw this opinion as a direct criticism of me as a person and my position as a parent. This has caused much conflict between my children and me. My own insecurities were much stronger than I ever gave them credit. It is after all so much easier to deal with an object. Hell, yes, you can place it down and unless you have fairies, it stays obediently put. I think about the things I did as a child, never once can I ever remember consciously thinking if I do this; that will piss them off and I do so want to piss them off for all the times it had been done to me. I realise now, all these years later, mostly kids are just kids. They say and do things not really comprehending the magnitude or significance of what they have done. I can hear some say," Oh yes the little shits do, some kids are just plain evil." That may be but then we all fit into that category at times, however children want to be loved and just be part of this large group, we as humans are naturally gregarious creatures. Some kids just do not have the right role models and then others for whatever reason take the wrong path, no different to many adults. I was once judged and was very hurt. But when I think back to Mr Cameron's words, "Young lady, come back to me when you are 35 and grown up" I realise one has to be more than 35 to be grown up sometimes; it is only in my mid fifties can I accept the person who judged me was speaking from their present knowledge not knowledge which was around 30 years ago. To accept criticism is maturity, knowing yourself worth and being confident in your own knowledge that is being a grown up. Allan not wishing to be cuddled and fussed over suited me. I felt that while I was not able to have this physical contact with my children I could make up for this inadequacy in other avenues. It has had a lasting effect on my children because I never did get the balance right. I can remember making a conscious decision when Mark was very small never to touch my children. I had read once that a person who was abused becomes the abuser. I was never going to put myself in that position where people might second guess my actions. I am amazed at the power of one's mind and am convinced that the witch doctor so many years ago was right but he underestimated and never understood my drive and determination to stop the abuse against the girl children in my line. I once told myself this abuse stops with me. I am so sure the baby I lost was a girl and so only ended up with two children. Until in late 90s Leah at 21 adopted us as her parents she calls us Ma and Pa Kettle.

I realised that a veggie garden on such a small size garden and children were not a very good combination. I levelled the vegetable garden after the second year and returfed the area to once again be a small cricket pitch. The plastic tubs which I had accumulated over time were used as substitute fielders on days when there were not enough kids to make up the teams. The upturned pots once hit by the batting person counted as caught and so the next person went into bat. Keith had a selection of second hand glass panes on hand ready to appease the neighbours as the cricket ball smashed through their glass houses where they housed their prize tomato plants. Keith showed his love for sport very early in his school life something neither of our two boys did seriously until they had left school. Keith played cricket for Hickling for a number of years while we lived in England. It was a sore point for many of his cousins all the time we lived there. Keith was adamant as they would not give him a fair go when we first arrived. He was not going to play for Long Clawson because it was once they realised his abilities did they invite him to play for them. Keith did say he could see their point after all who wants a no hoper in their team but did think he should have been given a chance. Allan preferred squash and played 'A' grade for a number of years once he had left school. Mark moved from archery to cycling to being an Iron Man. He completed the Foster's Iron Man while he served in the RAAF at 19.

Keith had a love-hate relationship with the snow. Working in the snow, when you jumped out of your vehicle to do a roadside repair on another, dropping waist deep into that icy cold white stuff was like being chased up a tree by a rhino. His love for it was he said it was a great leveller. Everyone's garden looked the same from the posh to the poorest. I loved the spring flowers the entire place was a wash of colour. People had planted crocuses in their lawns and as the snow melted so these delicate flowers popped up all over. In the Clawson Cover, the wild soft white snow drops with a small green dot were the perfect companion to the delicate wild purple violets. One year, the women from the Women's Institute of the village raised money and planted daffodils though out the entire village along the sidewalks. The next year showed its rewards we had the prettiest sidewalks with a carpet of yellow to mimic the sun which was a rare sight. The lack of the fierce African scorching sun did have its advantages the plants grew in such profusion one could not but find a new lease of life. Keith's mother did once say to me until I had tried new British spuds I had not lived they are truly amazing. They are quite sweet and unless you knew you were eating a spud you would think it another exotic vegetable there is an absence of that typically starchy taste. We have had an entire meal on a home grown lettuce; Warren, Keith's brother, said it was the most fantastic meal he had consumed in a long time.

Warren joined the Merchant Navy and spent his shore leave with us for the duration of his stay in England. Typical of a lot of the younger generation, he spent most of his spare time in the local pub with his younger friends. One night, he arrived home in a rather sad state. He had left his front door key at home. He tried climbing the drain pipe up to his room only thing the drain pipe was in the next door neighbour's yard. Eventually, he considered he would just have to wake us up. I was woken with a noise I got out of bed and felt sure it would be Warren but the absence of his cousin's car made me think otherwise then there was this horrendous banging on the front door. I went down and there stood Warren. I think at the sight of me he instantly sobered up. He was so apologetic all he kept saying was "Gees, Myrna, I am sorry. Gees, I am sorry, Myrna." The next morning, I asked him why he drank so much, what was in it for him? Warren told me when you drink you reach this euphoric plateau and the world was a beautiful place; that is until your sister-in-law opens the door for you. Poor Warren he was so afraid of me. I have a loathing for alcohol which has never weaned. It is so strong the very first time Keith came to pick me up at the Nurses Hostel one evening I smelt beer on his breath. I said accusingly, "You have been drinking!" He said that he had a beer with his dad at lunch; he was told if he ever wanted to see me again he had to give the drink up. I walked back into the nurse's hostel. For years, Keith never drank. I was so sure that anyone who had alcohol would instantly transform into the monster which I had grown up with. I have wondered about this for many years what was it that made me make the right choice in men both my sisters have attracted the same type of man that reflected my stepfather; they have had a number of partners and each one as poorer a choice as the last. Was it that I had told myself I would not accept this behaviour in a man or am I just one of the luckiest women this side of the Limpopo River? I certainly did break the statics mould.

Shortly after Warrens night out the two boys and I had that awful task of shopping for school clothes. Allan had a very definite idea of what he wanted but his taste did not match my pig's ears purse. He had what Trudy would have said was "a Champagne taste on a beer man's income." Frustration set in, I would not budge. Allan wanted a brand name pair of shoes which cost 120 pounds I tried to explain I could not justify spending that much money on one person in the family when his dad only got paid 67 pound a week. Eventually, I got fed up with his sulking and walked off. As I walked into a shop I looked round and he had not followed me into the store. I walked out and looked up and down the row of shops. Went back into the shop, collected Mark and I made my way back to the car. Allan was not there. I looked for an hour for him when I called the police. That is one thing which is truly amazing with the British police. We found they do not stop looking for kids until they found them one way or the other. Melton Mowbray had police cars criss-crossing the length and breadth of the place. I was in one squad car all the while they talked to each other. I gathered from the various conversations we had three cars out looking for Allan. At one point, there was a call that came in from the police station. Allan was at home. He had been picked up on the A46, the main highway between Melton Mowbray and Nottingham. Alice Wilford the Lady of the Manor was returning from doing some work at Sarson High School where she was the deputy head. Alice had recognised Allan on the road and stopped and she said to Allan, "Now then, my lad, get in this car and tell me what you are doing on this main road?" Allan told her I had just walked off and left him and he could not remember where the car was parked. Fortunately, Alice thought there was a little more to his story. When she arrived at home, she called the police station and asked if Allan had been reported missing. She was given the third degree. They wanted her driver's licence number her social security number before they were satisfied she was on the up and up. I am not sure whether the fact that just a week before a very young girl about the same age of Allan, 9 years old, went missing. She was found in the Hickling Woods, a village next to Long Clawson. The police had arrested a man who had played cricket with Keith and charged him with her murder. All the players were stunned. I was returned to my parked car and went home to find Keith and Allan. Keith was so angry with me for losing Allan in town. I refused to go with them to Allan's street fair instead I decided I needed to find a euphoric plateau. I drank an entire bottle of Cinzano Bianco Vermouth. I waited for the plateau which would make my world a beautiful place it never happened. I concluded I had not drunk enough but got bored with the exercise and felt so sorry for myself that I made my way up to bed. I managed to get halfway up the stairs when. Oh hell, what is happening, what have I done? My legs went from under me. I could not will them to work. I tried to call my brother by phone. Logically what was he going to do he was stuck in Croydon some 80 miles away. Logic has no place in a drunken stupor. I called my neighbour, she came over. In her broad *Leicestershire* accent she said, "What the fuck have you done? You are drunk, you silly bitch. Come on, let's get you into bed before the boys see you." I was so angry with Keith for taking as I had seen it sides against me I did not want to sleep in HIS BED. I was tucked up in the spare room. During the night, I threw up and it smelt of Cinzano. I peed the stuff. Keith asked me the following morning how did I feel. "You should know you have by all accounts been there more times than I have." As the day progressed, I realised all those years ago when my mother had said Adam was drunk so therefore did not know what he was doing. Beating us to within an inch of our lives; trying to have sex with his stepdaughter; LIES! Why would another human begin do this to children. Bull shit he did not know what he was doing. I had firsthand knowledge. I also knew what legless meant for the first and the last time. On very special occasions, like my 25 wedding anniversary, I will have a glass of wine. Two is my absolute limit. Keith says I will never get drunk again because I have to be in control of every situation. For me, it is the absolute dread of the hold alcohol is able to have on a person but also I can't stand the taste. On New Year, the whisky bottle is passed around so as not to offend Keith said just pretend to drink a sip. Whisky burns like fire going down perhaps the Red Indians knew more than the Whites gave them credit for calling alcohol Fire Water.

Who is Myrna

PAGE 1

FLORE WILLEM WOOT

BORN 11th AUGUST 1865? (YEAR NOT DEFINITE)
AT WILNES IN HOLLAND
H/AD 2 SISTERS + 1 BROTHER

QUALIFIED AS MASTER BUILDER
IN HOLLAND

WHEN 25 YEARS OLD AND HAD TO
SERVE IN NETHERLANDS FORCES
JOINED THE ARMY AND OPTED TO
SERVE OVERSEA

HIS BROTHER JOINED THE NAVY AND
WAS LOST AT SEA.

HIS SISTERS DID NOT MARRY AND
REMAINED IN HOLLAND (NOT DEFINITE, BUT
WHEN HE DIED MUM WROTE TO HIS SISTERS
AT LAST KNOWN ADDRESS BUT NEVER
RECEIVED A REPLY)

Page 2

He went to Netherlands East Indies in 1890 or there about and returned from there in 1912 or 1913.

When he reached the Cape not liking the news from home he left the ship at Cape Town and made his way to the then chartered territory of Rhodesia where he met and married Maria Magdelena Opperman.

While in the Far East he was stationed in various garrisons notably Batavia in Sumatra and Sowrabaya in Java.

He probably carried on his trade as Builder, not as a labourer, but more likely, as an overseer and trainer.

Although the call up period was for 5 years he stayed in the East for 20 years.

He probably did as most of the expatriates did. Took himself a common law wife.

PAGE 3

WHAT HAPPENED TO HER, IF THERE EVER WAS ONE, IS PROBLEMATICAL BUT I CAN'T SEE ANYBODY CUTTING HIMSELF OFF FROM HIS FAMILY WITHOUT GOOD REASONS, WHICH A EURASIAN FAMILY WOULD BE OF PRIMARY IMPORTANCE, BECAUSE HOWEVER LAX AND EASY-GOING THEY WERE IN THE COLONIES THEY WERE VERY STRICT AT HOME

AT THE TIME OF HIS DEATH THERE WAS SUPPOSED TO HAVE BEEN 30,000 GUILDER IN HOLLAND (PROBABLY PART OF HIS ARMY PAY) 1 GUILDER = 1/8d SO IF THE TOTAL AMOUNT WAS APPROX £2500 WHAT HAPPENED TO THIS I DON'T KNOW, BUT AT THE TIME IT WAS IMPOSSIBLE TO GO AND COLLECT IT AND TO MAKE ENQUIRIES AT LONG RANGE IS A SHEER WASTE OF TIME ESPECIALLY WHEN A LETTER WOULD TAKE ANYTHING UP TO 2 MTHS TO REACH ITS DESTINATION AND A REPLY, EVEN BY RETURN POST, AS LON

Page 14

So mum decided to laugh it off. So it is doubtful if there is any money anymore. Although as Willie is there, more or less on the spot, he might be able to institute enquiries.

Now of the Looit-Opperman connection there were 4 children 3 boys & 1 girl.

Floris Willem   Born 1.11.16
                Died 1981

Gotlieb Christian Rudolf (after his maternal grandfather   Born 18.10.17
                                                           Died 1987

Marinis Dirk (apparently Peter has 1 paternal aunt & uncle
                Born 25.6.19

Susanah Gertruida (after her maternal grandmother
                Born 11.8.20.

Floris Willem (snr) died Oct 1926 at Livingstone Zambia.

PAGE 3

Now from the known to the speculative.

According to family tales the name was originally Van Der Looit

Sometime in 1600 odd the head of the family Floris William V.D. Looit was left a widower

From the 1st marriage he had a son Floris William (it being a family name and all the 1st born boys was so named)

What other issue there was I don't know (but) they are not pertaining to the issue.

He married again and in due course his wife presented him with a boy then the trouble started.

The son from the 1st marriage was apparently then of age

His stepmother demanded that her son, being the 1st born of the 2nd family had an inalienable right to the family name. The older F. W. said "No How" or words to that effect. What part the father played is uncertain and a tho the old man was not

PAGE 6

VERY EXPLICIT

ANYWAY, THE OLDER F.W., HIMSELF BEING MARRIED, CONSIGNED HIS STEP MOTHER AND HER BROOD TO THE HOT PLACE, CHANGED HIS NAME TO LOOIT (WITHOUT THE VAN DER) AND DEPARTED.

ACCORDING TO THE OLD MAN (MY FATHER) THE V.D. LOOIT'S DIED OUT AFTER ABOUT 4 OR 5 GENERATIONS. I THINK WHAT PROBABLY HAPPENED IS THAT THERE WAS NO MALE ISSUE SO THE NAME V.D.L. FELL AWAY. IF THERE EVER WAS SUCH A FAMILY, I MIGHT BE WORTH TRACING IF POSSIBLE.

THIS IS PURELY SPECULATIVE. MY NAME "MARINIS" WOULD BE DERIVED FROM THE GREEK "MARINIS" (DOUBTFUL) OR FROM THE DUTCH "MARIJNA" (LITTLE MARY?) WHICH I UNDERSTAND WAS ONE THE NAME OF 1 OF HIS SISTERS.

NOW, BEARING IN MIND THAT THE LETTER "Y" DOES NOT OCCUR IN THE DUTCH ALPHABET TOGETHER WITH "Q" & "X" THE NAME "MYRNA" CAN ONLY BE A WRONGFUL SPELLING OF "MARIJNA" AS LOY IS A MISSPELLING OF LOOIT.

Page 7

We will now go back to the old man's probable Eurasian family.

Myrna Loy, the film star, is said to be of Javanese or Sumatran extraction.

She is about 71 years old so she was born just before or just after the O.M. left the East. I don't see him abandoning a wife and small child after 20 years so his wife was probably dead by that time and Myrna, if she was any real relation, would be a grandchild. Interesting theory.

When I named Myrna after the film star I forgot about the letter "Y" and I would probably have called her "Marina" whereas her name properly would have been Marina. Never mind.

The foregoing family history might be whole cloth made of unrelated threads, but one thing is definite. Willy was named after his grandfather Lodij — that his father had the same name is immaterial. Does well.

PAGE 8

was named after Grandfather Ockridan, Mum's father. Susan was named after Mum's mother, so I must have been named after Father Looit's mother. As we know Dad had a brother whose name we don't know, so I can't have been named after him. As alternate children was named after alternate grandparents families male & female in succession I must have been named after G.M. Looit and her name was Maria or a derivitive of that name of which Marina is one.

It is so very true. People see many of us as someone whom we don't always want to either accept as ourselves or recognise as being who we are. When I was nine years old many years before my father's letter was written, I remember I would stand in front of the mirror and talk to whom I believed was my great aunt Myrna Loy. I drew a lot of strength from this great lady in times when I felt so alone. I thought one day I too would be a great lady. An air of confidence would fill the mirror and my pride would swell the more I spoke to her. Many years later I read her biography only to read her name was given to her by a poet and was a pseudonym. I did so want to write to her and tell her how she had helped me through my childhood believing her to be my great aunt; however she was portrayed as a very private person and I felt I should respect her for that. Perhaps it was this confidence and pride which enveloped me which my mother interpreted as arrogance, conceit or self-importance which resulted in her nickname for me "Lady Jane". I was told by her that it was a result of thinking I was better than the family. That childhood pride and confidence soon was a distant memory never to rear its head later on not in my teenage years or adulthood.

I am convinced when I once asked Keith, "Please, let me find out for myself." Stems from not having had the interaction with my parents most children had. There has been much research done to try and establish what is 'learned behaviour' and what is 'inherent'. Most animals, the ones whom have not been allowed to interact with their own species their journey in their life some say only start when they are reintroduced back into their own environment with their own kind instead of that journey starting at birth. Apes who have been hand raised do not understand the social order and are very often shunned, bullied, if not killed before they learn how to behave. Humans suffer the same fate when they are forbidden to experience certain aspects of things many of us take for granted. My upbringing was so strict, we were never allowed to interact with others. Never allowed to grow through our own expressions and learn from those mistakes. I am convinced I do not wear makeup because of this fundamental reason. I was never allowed to experiment with it as a child. Consequently, I do not know how to apply the stuff so that I do not look like the Christmas tree I was once referenced to. People remark on how much younger I look than my actual age. I think this is partly to do with I have never worn makeup which has destroyed much of the skin's natural ability to repair itself. Also some people just have young genes. Look at Cliff Richard, how young does he still look. There is another fact that I am convinced, adults do not have the resilience children have. You can recover from a lot as a child but should you be presented with those same circumstances as an adult, you don't recover fairing so well. I have been the lady of my house and never had a hard married adult life. One of my siblings was asked how much younger is Myrna to you.

As I have grown older, I think more and more about why I behave or have certain opinions. I see myself as a very strong person, someone who always will try and do her best. I am very shy in a crowd and will always be the person at a party whom you will find in the kitchen quietly going about cleaning. Keith says I always believe that all people are good and there are no bad people in the world. Hence, the reason I will always stop to help anyone. I once told a shrink that if I was to die helping someone, what an honourable way to die. His reply was I was a very selfish person what would happen to my family if I was dead. I believe in most instances our lives are preordained certainly the day we die and are born is out of our hands. I know there are bad people but I choose not to accept that they are all bad. There is good in everyone.

Others have said I am a bully, and if things don't go my way, I sulk. I do have a very short fuse, but once it is out of my system, I tend to think I move on. I have never seen myself as someone who sulks.

We were living in England when I realised, my mother had lied to me. I was so badly affected, I so desperately wanted to talk to someone about how very let down and hurt I was. Why did she do it, what was her motive. It was not until much later in Australia when I had the inevitable break down was I able to talk to someone. The breakdown was inevitable my GP, Peter, spoke to me through rivers of tears in his surgery one day he said, "Myrna, you kid yourself, you have not coped with life, you have muddled your way through your life and now this muddling has come undone. It is time now that you get things sorted and it will take a long time of careful counselling because you have left it for so long." (Not my fault had I not been brainwashed into thinking there will never be any help for me. 'What happens at home stays at home.') Peter is the best doctor I have ever had the pleasure of talking to, he listened, a rare trait in many professional people. He once asked me what is it about you people from Africa that you have to drive yourself to the point of total exhaustion before you will concede.

I went home and thought about that statement and came to the conclusion; because I see myself as an ambassador to Zimbabwe, I can't allow anyone to see any flaws in me for fear that all Zimbabweans are being judge by my actions. We are already behind the eight ball how useless are we, as a nation, we could not hold on to our own country. Be that rational or not it is how I think. There will be people who can't possibly understand that. Zimbabwe was a country that was judged by people who might never have set foot in the country and yet they saw fit to change what seems like an eternity, a whole life time of work. I was third generation and had lived through the breakup of the Federation of Southern Rhodesia, Northern Rhodesia and Nyasaland. We had seen how the granting of independences was badly managed all around our boarders, Europeans were being tossed out of these countries a place they had only know as home all of their life and for some their parent's life.

I think of countries like America what if the Red Indians had banded together and driven the Europeans from their shore line all those years ago or even Australia. The unspeakable atrocities which we as Europeans did to the natives of these countries are unforgivable. I saw Rhodesia as a very moderate and tolerant country. For these beliefs I joined the march to say sorry to the Aboriginals, not because I had personally done them harm but as a member of the human race we had wronged another. I often reflect on what made Africa and its countries so different to these two countries, why did Great Britain have this sudden burst of conscience, why was she so hell bent on fixing the wrongs she had done all in a matter of a few months. Europe had taken hundreds of years to get through to what we all now concede is a civilised world yet she was asking African states to do it in less than two hundred years.

This brings up another point for me what is it that drives one person to relentlessly try and succeed where another might just say well I am thought to be useless so therefore I am. Adam constantly told me that I was that useless I would not even make a good useless housewife. I have been driven by his statement all my life. Why? I have not worked it out yet. Why can some people see a mess and have this compulsion to clean it while other may see it but are able to leave it or even not be aware they have made a sticky mess. Is this an extension of my personality type "rescuer." I am so driven by this obsession, to the point that I go into a total melt down, not able to function for a split second when someone especially a child presents themself to me who I see as needing rescuing. This I think and believe to stem from when I looked after Gretha and she went to hospital for malnutrition. I have been asked to do some research into malnutrition to try and work through this feeling of being responsible for Gretha. I have found research which does talk about how long a child has to be without food to become malnourished. I however know what I said to myself all those years ago. I said, "Well, Gretha you will eat when you get hungry." I let her get on with it. I, as a ten-year-old was always eating because I was always hungry so why would a three-year-old not be driven to eat when they were hungry. I blame myself for being lazy and not making her eat. My other thought was after all if she did not eat, one less to have to find food for. I have been asked what is it with you everyone and everything has to eat. I grow food especially for birds in my garden. My home is never without food and something nice to eat. Caterpillars if they are found on a favourite plant are just relocated onto a shrub or flower which might be more robust to withstand their veracious appetite. If anyone says anything to me about this I brush it away with, if we kill all the caterpillars we will soon have no butterflies or moths. The truth is, I have this overwhelming compulsion to make sure everything and everyone has food.

Some may see the personality type of rescuer being a damaging personality, for me, I embrace it. Helping others and thinking of your fellow human being is not a bad thing. More of us should do it. It has cost me at times more than I was able to give. It has seen a rift grow between Gretha and me so large it may never be closed. However, I continue to prefer my giving side and will guard, nurture, and show it off proudly forever. As with all things in life, I have to learn how to moderate this side of my personality. All things in moderation are good.

Another topic which came up in our sessions was Willy once said to me that my mother had offered me to Adam when she could no longer cope with his insatiable appetite for sex. I also recalled that she herself was abused by her own father. Adam one day found this out and beat this man up. I at the time I could not comprehend this because the very thing that repulsed him he was doing. I was horrified at Willy's suggestion that a mother would actually do this to her child. Trying to understand these actions during a visit to the shrink the dealing of the Jews by Hitler was brought to the discussion. Humans when they find themselves in what must have been the most life threatening situation will look to whatever survival skills they have. Perhaps likewise, we were all trying to just make it through to the next day alive not unlike their plight must have been. I am not sure and if Willy is correct in his recollection of events or not but I believe it did not occur and for me it is my mom's saving grace. However, if she did, I forgive her. My self belief in humans, if given a choice we would not act badly. Combined with my compassionate side which takes over, I look at who she was and what tools were at her disposal had she not suffered the same fate at the hands of her father? I believe my mom's own self awareness, knowledge, and comprehension of worldly matters never evolved to this plane of understanding. I think the reason lies in the fact my mother did not see the harm it had caused her in her life and did not see it as harmful as we now know this type of abuse to be. I too would not be damaged. Her actions if they were as my brother suggested were done out of a consciousness for survival. The statement which sticks in my mind was once Adam was attacking us physically and my mom stepped in and said, "Please, rather hit me than my kids." Is this the actions of a woman who had offered her own daughter up to a man like Adam? I cannot believe it and so it still is and always will be for me her saving grace. Of all the things my parents did wrong I have held on to that instance all my life. I truly believe if she had the power to change things she would have. She was doing a self preservation of her own life in a most violent situation.

When I recall the instances when our servants stepped in to protect us as children, I can give you the house we lived in and what proceeded and escalated to the violence but not that much detail when it comes to my mom the day she stepped in and recued me from Adam. I now wonder if this did take place or did I want this incident to happen that much it only happened in my imagination and dreams.

I was called for Jury Duty. This was great. It gave me a sense of patriotism. I felt proud to do my civic duty to my new country. I felt truly it might help to cement a feeling which I should have towards being a part of this great wonderful place I now call home. All was running smoothly until in the docks sat a middle aged man accused of sexually assaulting a young girl. Only now they give it some fancy term which means nothing like the horrific crime itself. The man was charged with; 'repeated acts of lewdness and showing a minor pornographic videos'. I remember standing at the back of the court room while they read the charges out just before they picked the jury and thought, "What the hell does that mean," just say what it is, 'sexual assault.' It is nothing pretty, it does not deserve to be wrapped in fancy words.

As I took stock of the court room the lay out looked the same as the one I had found myself in so many years ago. My heart began to race. I felt angry and sick, I gripped my stomach in the hopes the pain would go away; would I be able to do this civic duty? I stared at the man in the docks he must have walked in with the aid of a cane; it hung like a crippled war veteran's cane hooked over the chair so as to make everyone think of all their grandfathers, uncles, and dads who might have fought in a war. I felt nothing but contempt for this man and saw his cane as a pathetic futile effort to try and sway the jury to have some compassion for him. I was drawn into the proceedings as the man next to me got up as his name was called.

Each side selected who they thought would best aid their case. The prosecution called middle aged men and women, more men; the Defence called younger citizens and more women than men. Then what followed shocked me beyond belief. Why was this still happening? For shits sake is there ever going to be someone who will protect the children? Why did the mother give permission for the child to be crossed examined? Have these children not suffered enough? The remainder of the jury were dismissed.

I walked to work with this overwhelming sadness in my heart. I was angry and so sad for the child. If she was mine, that man would not have made it to court he would have died by my hand and rightly so. I arrived at work shaking like a volcanic mountain before its eruption. I walked into the manager's office and said I could not work today. I was in such a state, I had to be driven home. I remember stating my stepfather did 12 months for what he did when was my sentence ever going to end?

I was no better the next day and went to see Peter. He said, Myrna, the next time you get a letter to do Jury Duty you have to bring it to me, this has nothing to do with your patriotic duty, it is about self preservation and not wasting tax payers money what if you had been chosen as a member of the jury and your past experience only came home to you say two days into trial. The potential damage it could have done to me and the trail might have been irreparable. Peter said there is sadly members of our community who will never and should never do jury duty and I was sadly one of those people. I said, "Well, I should imagine I won't get another now for some years." Peter was not so sure. Three months later I received another summons to appear for jury duty. Peter true to his word wrote them a letter and said under no circumstances was I ever to be called for jury duty due to a past medical history.

My continued sentence was to once again surface in 2004. It took many months and almost three years for me to understand. My philosophy in life has been if one can understand, one can accept and move on to hopefully a better place, a more productive time. I realised on 27 March 2007, why an email which I was sure started my rollercoaster downward spiral into a very deepest state of depression. I had allowed it to render me unfit for work for almost 6 months the poem had such a profound impact on me. It was during my session with the shrink I came to the realisation I was what in their world is labelled a 'rescuer.' It was this part of my personality which was my undoing when I read the chain email.

"My name is Sarah,
I am three
and last night
my Daddy murdered me".

I had been trying to search for a reason, "Why did my wheels fall off my bus?" Being sure if I could only understand why, I would be able to forgive myself; this feeling that I had let myself down and others around me. Professional people who have tried to help me through this period have said it was because I had many triggers and stressors hitting simultaneously. I could not accept this. I have in the past been able to deal with many stressors which make up my day, week or month. The understanding of what went wrong came to me as I was completing a project at work. I found a payment of 14 thousand and was flabbergasted at how this payment did not make the Accrual Register. I then began to think about the time this payment happened and realised it was around the period I was on a return to work restricted duties programme. I talked to a colleague about what I felt was the plausible reason for this over sight. She said, "Yes. I heard that you were returning to work after a long illness, why were you off work"?

I said that I had received one of these chain emails and I was totally derailed. As I recited the last verse of the poem the light was slowing getting brighter. I was totally aware of why I was in such a state. For the first time since Christmas 2004, I had an answer which I could accept. Sarah was one child I will never be able to rescue. Death is final. It is the end of a life which can never be brought back. Previously I had asked myself, why did I just want to give up, this is not like me. Why did I think I no longer wanted to be a part of this place? I thought of how cruel we were as a human race, we do the meanest things to one another and I did not want to be a part of it any more. During those first few months, I had pondered why do people write notes when they leave, No one really gives a shit, I was adamant when I do leave I will not write a note. The salty floods had striped the glazing off my glasses. I am not sure why I did not leave, I had plenty of opportunities I was alone in the house for a number of months. My shrink asked me to promise her once that I would see her at our next weekly visit. I am sure they ask this of all their patients. Peter asked me if he needed to put me in hospital. I was quite shocked at this I asked him if he was nuts. He said, "No, you are!" "Why would I want to go to hospital, I am not sick, you fool!" Peter said, "Just you remember you told me you were not sick." Several months went by before I realised what he meant by being put into hospital he wanted me on 'suicide watch.' Leah was the only person who would make a point of coming over and making sure I was OK. At times, it was her weekly visits which would see me have a meal. I gave a lot of my very personal things away not trusting others to do what I would like. Not trusting myself to take another blow. Leah was given a gold painted coffee set which my mother gave me when I left home at 15. The set had travel from Africa to England and finally to Australia. Ironically, Adam had won it in a darts game at the Glass Castle Hotel in Bulawayo. I was now thinking of the very best home for my coffee set. It became mine through the actions of a man who had done so much damage and yet it was amongst my prize passions. My mother gave it to me and said it was to remember her. I have told Leah it is to go to my granddaughter on her twenty-first birthday. I was not sure I would still be around then.

During one of my fortnightly visits to the shrink, I was given a book to read, *Taming the Black Dog* by Bev Aisbett. I took it to Peter on one of my off weekly visits to the shrink and we discussed it. Winston

Churchill had episodes of depression. I don't really remember too much of the book other than I interpreted it to make the inference; when you take all the trimmings away all the emotional pain and you are totally honest with yourself, depression was a state of *self pity; inactivity; wanting to be rescued; blaming others/life for your situation; wanting to be looked after and or wanting to be in control of others.* I remember when reading this I said to Peter hell is that all depression is, shit I can beat this. I had never thought I felt self pity; I was not going to start now. The rest of it 'inactivity' it was the chicken egg scenario for me. 'Wanting to be rescued' don't we all feel like that from time to time. 'Blaming' we all do this when things have not gone the way we thought they ought to it seem like something which was just part of who we are. 'Being looked after' we are gregarious by nature and therefore it is an expectation as far as I could see; what is wrong with wanting to be looked after if you are of such a large social order. The last one this was tough; in all the self-help books they tell you to own your own destiny is that not the same as wanting to control others and the situation to your own ends. I felt the only one was self pity that I could understand and fix. Depression is such a complex condition and I truly believe not many doctors understand its complexities fully hence the number of people who still feel suicide is their only way out. It took me a number of months and eventually I did have to take medication. Something I fought long and hard not to take. My shrink was so concerned about my mental state Keith was given the prescription and we only had a few days' supply at a time in the house. I have a very serious stumbling block about medication of any kind. It goes something like; "In the year 25 25 if man is still alive, everything we think, do and say is in the pill we took today". The one hit wonder by Zager and Evans.

I truly hope this helps people think more responsibly about how they talk and what they say to each other. We really do not know what cross each and every one of us carry and if it might be our actions which serves to push that last red button and explode the atom bomb in anyone of us. Please be kind to each other. We only have each other. No man is an island. I have on occasions attended a number of workshops during my working career both externally and internally and on two separate occasions I have heard a statement which says we as in 'I can't be held responsible for how another person processes information.' I have stood up and always will and say that is "*total bull shit*". Each and every one of us is responsible for our fellow human being. We also know through our own feelings what is hurtful and can if we thought more about the other person instead of ourselves we would be able to anticipate how they might well process particular information. It goes back to that old aged proverb "do unto other as you have done unto you" Unfortunately, we now live in a society which does not believe in taking responsibility and suffer the consequences of one's own actions.

I still feel resentment towards the government firm I worked for. They have a code of conduct which when needed to be enforced is mostly not followed through. Instead they rewarded the person who sent the email with a promotion from an Administration Office level 2 to a level 5 within the 6 months I was fighting for my very life. The people around me, my manager, the work environment officer, and the union I belonged to, who were supposed to protect workers against other staff who did not obey and adhere to the code of conduct, I felt these staff members did not do their jobs very well. The code of conduct says sending chain emails is forbidden and can result in dismissal. I did bring this particular email to my manager's attention. However, I did not follow the correct process and completed the correct forms it was never recorded as an official complaint. I did at one time think of taking them to task through a court process but I was not emotionally strong enough to do this on my own. I instead went through a process of a Work Cover Tribunal with a union rep who did not know how the system or perhaps it was always her intention to be half an hour late. Once the meeting at a Tribunal has started, no one can join the meeting. I would have been left out in the cold had the previous meeting not run over time. She also advised me to take a medical redeployment out of that department. A medical redeployment is a system where the department has an obligation to find you another position within the establishment within 12 months and if no such position can be found you forfeit your permanent status. This translated means you are without a job. I felt at the time I had lost so much, why too must I now put myself in a position where I could potentially lose my job? A job so well done I was one of twelve finalist state wide nominated to receive an award of excellence at Parliament House. Some years later I was again nominated and won an award of excellence when the government had a reshuffle and I worked for the smaller department Accommodation Services and Respite Support. The saddest thing is I have observed a number of staff hit rock bottom at work because management have not enforced the code of conduct and then the staff have had to pick themselves up and just move on or move out. In reality, their code of conduct is very rarely enforced. We continually have severe cases of work place bulling and harassment, it goes on in all of government departments and I should think if it goes on within my work place realistically it is rife throughout the our entire lifestyle. I look at the futile efforts of the schools trying to stamp out bulling they have no hope while we as adults do it to each other.

Keith's nickname for me has been 'Myrna the Learner' and I like to think I am always learning.

Albert Einstein quoted

"Learn from yesterday, live for today, hope for tomorrow. The important thing is not to stop questioning".

I have always read a lot of self-help books and realised that while every one of them has something to say each of us must sift through what is written and take whatever make sense to us but also not disregard the rest but store it. I also read very slowly so will only read books that I can get something out of. In the list of books I have read, especially in the self-help category, a common thread is the mind is all powerful. So powerful there is still much work to be done to fully understand it. Some go so far as to say if you think it your brain will conjure up a situation as to bring about what your inner thoughts are. I have always advocated one must never wish others ill your brain does not know who 'Joe Soap' is but it does only know you so it thinks you personally would like to be in that situation. I remember when Keith asked me to marry him I replied with "Are you sure about this because my children will never see the inside of a children's home." (From that statement one might think I had regrets with my choice to go to the Home; nothing could be further from the truth) Was this idea or mindset buried in my subconscious somewhere or was I just extremely lucky in that wide sea of partners to be chosen by Keith. There is a lot of statistical evidence about which will show people choose partners which will result in them reliving their childhood.

I read mostly autobiographies. One such book was *A Fortunate Life*. I read how this man stayed so positive throughout his life. It gives me courage to strive to be the best that I can. I do think about Adam's statement about being so useless why some of us tell ourselves I'll show you I am not useless. Others are just as strong willed. They say, you say I am so therefore I will show you how useless I can be. I do watch a lot of movies and appear to get more from this entertainment than others. I will question. I wonder what made whoever writes that story line; did they take it from life experiences. Keith says it is just a movie. Yes, but where did the idea come from. Every story retold has an element of truth or fact in it is my philosophy. Even science fiction which is not my cup of tea has at times a message in it.

I watched a movie with Nicole Kidman and Tom Cruise *Eyes Wide Shut*. In the 1970s, we consulted a doctor about permanent sterilisation. I was 23 and had three pregnancies. Most certainly did not want another pregnancy or any more children. They took one look at my age and said absolutely not. The only other solution was to visit an urologist. It was suggested many men were not able to cope with sterilisation. They were thought not to be emotionally and sexually mature. Somehow being sterilised took their manhood away. This was further embellished by the doctor when he said he is often asked by would be patients, "Will my beard stop growing and or will I speak with a squeaky voice?" A man's masculinity is very fragile. The element of truth used in this movie. Nicole tells Tom of her fantasy dream. He is so emasculated, he peruses what he sees as his own inadequacies and lands himself in a whole heap of pain. A documented statistic perhaps in some journal and with some clever thought and imagination it has been used in a movie.

John Winslow Irving (born John Wallace Blunt, Jr) who wrote *The Cider House Rules* written in 1985 and made into a movie in 1999 builds his story on some very serious facts and makes reference to Fetal Alcohol Syndrome (first theorised and studied in the US by physicians, David W. Smith and Kenneth L. Jones in scientific literature in The Lancet in 1973. It was previously described in France in 1968 by Paul Lemoine.) He says he has noticed those women who drink during pregnancy, their babies suffer. Homer suggests it is only a cold. It is later revealed the X-rays showing a heart condition does not belong to Homer but Fuzzy Stone, (Erik Per Sullivan) who played the orphan whom Dr. Larch had referenced to as suffering from weak lungs and a heart condition.

There are not too many fictional novels which do not have an element of truth/fact in them somewhere; after all life is much stranger than fiction. My way of thinking is everything we experience is a source of learning we can never dismiss anything.

When we first arrived in England, we were compared to a coiled spring. Keith unfortunately has never been able to uncoil his spring and soon displayed what we now know to be Post Traumatic Stress Disorder. We did not make the connection. How did I not see it? In old war movies it was called shell shock. Keith found himself in a very similar situation as some men have been portrayed in movies where they dive for cover from imaginary bombings. Walking to work one morning a tractor tire burst, in one single motion Keith cleared a four foot mud wall and leopard crawled to safety. He later relayed his incident but laughed it off and we all laughed at him.

For Keith, his world is black and white. The army training he received reinforced that way of thinking and that is the law he lives by. This thinking has proved very difficult to live with but mostly for him. In Keith's world, he was to be the provider for his family and since leaving Zimbabwe he feels that he has not done this very well. In Zimbabwe, he only ever worked for two firms but since, in Australia alone he has had 9 jobs in 17 years. He gave up on the workforce in 2004.

Despite having lived in three different countries, having a home which is almost paid off, we own our cars outright for Keith the glass will always be half empty. At one point, I did ask him why he could not look to the man who once came to his school all those years ago. If Douglas Bader was to have the feelings that he had; would he have been able to achieve the extraordinary feats in his life? Keith's answer was, "good for him!" Is it really just as simple as a personality choice or do we indeed have a choice when it comes to our own personalities. During a dark period in our marriage, it was felt that had I not have made him leave Zimbabwe he would not suffer from PTSD. I have done some research to try and understand this condition and he might well be right. It is well documented in every instance where men have been able to stay and rebuild what they see as something they have had a hand in destroying they have fared better than those who left immediately following the aftermath. The returning Vietnam Veterans who were shipped out from Vietnam had days where they were able to debrief each other and come to terms with the horrors they had encountered. The men who have shown more significant signs of trauma were flown out of Vietnam and supposedly home safe within a matter of hours.

Doug Burke who was once a counsellor with the Vietnam Veterans said the war Keith fought in was far worse than many of the wars. Keith's pattern in the last years of that war was 6 weeks in the bush 10 days at home. Every stint Keith was switched on, but he was never switched off. He compared that to be stood up against a wall and told today we are going to shoot you. Make you endure that stance for however long and then say, "No today is your lucky day." The exercise however without warning was repeated another day.

For Keith, it was in 10 days time when he was to endure more human suffering his poem 'Soldier's Lament' describes some of those horrors he faced. Working through PTSD is a constant challenge and we work with him every day being mindful that a sudden noise will send him into a sudden panic. When we go out for a meal, we need to find the table which has a seat with his back to a wall so that he can see his enemy coming from a long way off. Dimly lit places might be a romantic spot for most, for Keith it is a place that can produce too many surprises. Crowed places are a market for a terrorist bomber. There are too many people to watch, too many noises to decipher, not a good place to be. Watching him in a place like this reminds me of a mother hen trying desperately to shield her chicks from a hawk. Only, poor Keith, the enemy is not only above but all around him. His eyes are everywhere, his body is constantly twitching, he is in this heighten state of alert and readiness. To watch someone like that makes even the calmest and most relaxed person nervous we do not go to any place where there are a lot of people.

I pulled the plug at going to Speedway when I realised what and why he was doing what he did. I did try and say if we stayed seated until everyone had left but this never suited him either, there would be too many people milling round his space. Keith would have to leave long before the last race; where was the fun in that it was always in the last race most of the excitement happened it was like getting to the end of a thriller and finding someone had torn the last page out or taken the last jigsaw piece and hidden it; just to steal your thundering triumph of the satisfaction, standing back and looking at the finished puzzle.

I have a very simplistic and perhaps a naive approach. War is a despicable act and will bring out every human failure and at times bring some amazing surprises. Should we be able to accept this many would not suffer from PTSD. After all, we live in a world where we lay blame at someone else's feet most of the time. Perhaps my idealism would change if I was forced to see or indeed behaved as many of the men have had to so as to keep their loved ones safe as so many of them were told they were fighting for a better world.

One subject matter which has held a fascination for me is human behaviour. I wish I could study people much like Dian Fossey an American zoologist, primatologist, and anthropologist who undertook an extensive study of mountain gorilla groups.

Why do I feel I have to have approval from others to feel good? Is it only me or are other people in the same boat. I looked this up on the internet. (Fantastic tool)

One site—Inward Quest .com suggested

"It all boils down to the desire to feel loved and appreciated. For most people in the world approval-seeking is an expression of low self-esteem. Praise temporarily fills the void created by the feeling of not being loved and we experience pleasant emotions. Because we don't know how to close this void we figure that we can only be happy when others approve of us. Usually we come to this conclusion when we are still very little because the big people around us that we look up to (parents, teachers etc.) are fond of harshly expressing their disapproval when we don't act the way they expect us to. Disapproval feels bad so we start trying to act in a way that others will like and gradually this kind of behaviour becomes a habit. Slowly the emotional high we get from approval becomes addictive and when we don't get our dose, we suffer. That motivates to conform to others' rules even more. As with any disturbing emotion though, approval-seeking too can be transformed into something useful. If we could let go of the craving for it, receiving or not receiving approval can be a valuable guide, that shows us whether we are offering something of value or not. If people are not up-voting my answer, it's because it's not valuable to them.

There are many techniques to eliminate low self-esteem but to really close the void we have to raise our awareness and see that the very energy from which we originate is loving and kind and being omnipresent it is all around us and even in us all the time. There is no reason to feel unloved ever".

Shane Ferguson Psychologist a work colleague offered this explanation:

It's a primitive function, which comes back to the root of civilisation. There is actually a centre in the brain for pleasure that becomes more active when we get validated; so it's kind of inbuilt

I can relate to the first suggestion approval has become an addiction for me and why because Theron always said, "I was that useless I would not even be able to be a good useless housewife." Tell a child this often and they have that image ingrained into their brain. I do however now think having read this section, I have another skill to add to my coping strategies question why another has not given me that craving approval. It might be just simply because it is not valuable to them. Not how good or poorly I have performed in doing the set task.

When I lived in the Childrens' Home we had a number of different House Managers/Superintendent; I remember one in particular Mrs. Tilbrook. She at the time was considered a forward thinking person but as I later learned not always right in her thinking. Members of the board regretted appointing her. That is the way it is in life one thinks a certain way and imparts that knowledge or thought onto our own without giving it too much consideration and like a self help book each of us must draw knowledge and wisdom from life itself. Mrs. Tilbrook stopped all the children from going to the regular dress rehearsal of the eisteddfod. (in the then Salisbury Harare). Her thought was because the Home was run on charity why should we the children not be given more than a mere token. She felt we ought to have been given tickets to see the real deal anything else was an insult

One day Keith moved a concrete slab for me it really was far too big to be moved. I insisted. 'Where there was a will there was a way.' We dug down the sides to see if it was set into the ground or just laying on the top. We moved the sucker just as some say the stones for the pyramids might have been moved. The problem was the underside was rough and would not move very easily so with no further consideration to Myrna the Learner we had to turn it upside down. This done, we moved the slab to the spot I now wanted it but the dilemma now was the space was confined and not so easy to turn it right side up. In the process, the slab broke. I am somewhat of a perfectionist the slab was broken I did not want it now. I told Keith as much. What I learnt from this lesson was Mrs. Tilbrook was wrong in refusing the Dress Rehearsal Tickets to the Eisteddfod. Perhaps it was not her choice of the best but it was the best the organisation could do at the time.

Keith was so hurt by my lack of graciousness. He stormed off and said, "I bloody told you the thing was too big to be moved." I wrote and told Mrs Klette of my revolutionary lesson in life. You cannot and should never criticise someone for helping you even if the end product is not exactly as you wanted it.

witchdoctor's predictions

   a. I was to marry a foreigner;
   b. Should like two children but will have three;
   c. My family and I were to go over many waters.

My life thus far:

   a. I married a foreigner;
   b. I have two boys and miscarried a third child;
   c. My family and I have live in three very different countries; many miles away from the previous one.

Coincidence; was the witch doctor really all knowing or was it the power of suggestion deeply rooted in my subconscious that has shaped my life?